Art Nouveau

Posters & Illustration from the Glamorous Fin de Siècle

Publisher and Creative Director: Nick Wells
Project Editor and Picture Research: Sara Robson
Art Director and Layout Design: Mike Spender and Jake
Digital Design and Production: Chris Herbert

Special thanks to: Frances Bodiam, Chelsea Edwards, Cat Emslie, Anna Groves, Rebecca Kidd,
Victoria Lyle, Sam Shore and Helen Tovey

Fall River Press
122 Fifth Avenue
New York, NY 10011

ISBN: 978-1-4351-1770-9

Printed and bound in China

1 3 5 7 9 10 8 6 4 2

ART NOUVEAU

Posters & Illustration from the Glamorous Fin de Siècle

ROSALIND ORMISTON & MICHAEL ROBINSON

FALL RIVER PRESS

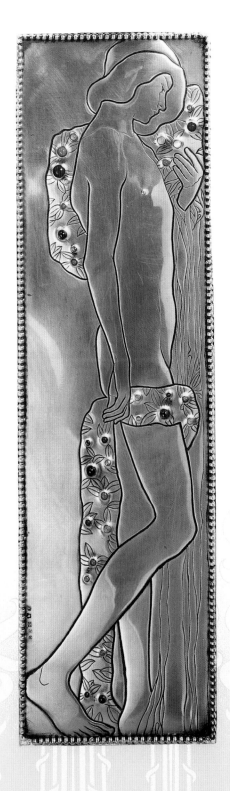

CONTENTS

INTRODUCTION

The age of Art Nouveau was an unprecedented epoch in the decorative, fine and graphic arts, a fusion of disparate philosophical and artistic ideas that found its apogee in Continental Europe and America. The general consensus is that its origins lay in the ideology and aesthetic of the British Arts and Crafts movement and that it was manifest as a style between 1894 and the outbreak of the First World War, although it had considerably waned after about 1905.

The art historian Nikolaus Pevsner (1910–83), in his *Pioneers of Modern Design* (first published 1936), suggests that the first flowering of the Art Nouveau style, with its curvilinear forms, can be traced to a drawing by the British Arts and Crafts pioneer Arthur Heygate Mackmurdo (1851–1942) in 1883. These same forms with their sinuous lines can also be seen in the work of the Pre-Raphaelite painter Edward Burne-Jones (1833–98) and his protégé Aubrey Beardsley (1872–98) in the early 1890s. In the case of Mackmurdo (and other Arts and Crafts practitioners) these sinuous lines are often based on plant forms, as advocated by the great writer on aesthetics, John Ruskin (1819–1900), who advised artists to 'go to nature' for their inspiration. Examples of their work and their ethos, together with the ideas and philosophies of William Morris (1834–96) and Ruskin, were promulgated in a journal published monthly from 1893 called *The Studio*, which was avidly read across Europe.

In Continental Europe, many artists had become disillusioned with the rigorous, conservative values of academic training and art practice that pervaded their respective countries. They identified a problem in the slavish mimesis of historicist elements, particularly those of the Renaissance and Classicism. Groups of artists in several cities broke away from their respective academies to set up what became known as '*Secessions*'. The first of these was in Munich in 1892, followed by Vienna in 1897 and Berlin in 1898. There were, however, earlier precedents to Art Nouveau forms in Europe that included the group known as '*Les Vingt*'. These were a group of 20 artists, mainly Belgians, who took their inspiration from Symbolist and Neo-Impressionist ideas, forming their group as early as 1884. Among their group was the young Henry van de Velde (1863–1957), who joined in 1888 and later epitomized Belgium's contribution to the Art Nouveau style. The group's journal *L'Art Moderne* first coined the term stating that 'we are believers in *art nouveau* (the new art)'. However, the term is usually associated with the opening of a gallery in Paris by Siegfried (a.k.a. Samuel) Bing (1838–1905) in 1895, La Maison de l'Art Nouveau. Bing was a German *émigré* who had experience of the ceramics trade, travelled to Japan in 1875, and opened his first shop in 1877 called La Porte Chinoise. Essentially he had a love for the Rococo designs of the eighteenth century and was also instrumental in publicizing Japanese artefacts in a journal called *Artistic Japan* in the late 1880s. Bing was one of many artists and Aesthetes who eagerly collected Japanese ephemera and promoted the aesthetic of simple line and colour in graphics that also eschewed notions of perspective. The idea of his new gallery was to bring together a number of artefacts from various sources that together would create a vogue for the new (*nouveau*) art forms, in designed objects, paintings and graphics. He commissioned Louis Comfort Tiffany (1848–1933) to create stained-glass windows for his gallery, as well as selling his glassware. Bing introduced British Arts and Crafts objects and paintings by Walter Crane (1845–1915), Morris and William Benson (1854–1924). Many of these objects contained aspects of the Art Nouveau style, particularly in the work of Crane, but it was really the designed objects by Tiffany, René Lalique (1860–1945), and van de Velde who gave impetus to the curvilinear forms that created the aesthetic synonymous with Art Nouveau.

The aesthetic and philosophical design ideas associated with Art Nouveau, that is the notion of a 'new art' for a new and progressive age, circulated around Europe in a number of journals and spawned varying interpretations of the style. The German art historian and polemicist Julius Meier-Graefe (1867–1935) started a journal called *Pan*, circulated from 1894, and later *Dekorative Kunst* in Munich. These journals continued to wax lyrical about the British Arts and Crafts practitioners, but also introduced people to what was happening in various cities. Meier-Graefe also opened his own gallery in Paris called La Maison Moderne designed by van de Velde, along similar lines to Bing's, a showcase for modern and up-to-date design. Van de Velde moved to Germany in 1900 where their equivalent Art Nouveau movement had taken hold called *Jugendstil*, after the journal *Jugend* that had been published to promote the new style from 1896.

The year 1900 saw the apogee of the style at the *Exposition Universelle* held in Paris, which brought together the different interpretations of Art Nouveau. Bing had his own pavilion with graphics, fine art and designed objects on display by many of the most-famous practitioners of Art Nouveau, including Alphonse Mucha (1860–1939), Henri de Toulouse-Lautrec (1864–1901), Tiffany and Lalique. Probably the most notable exhibit at the exposition was the new underground-train system. The entranceways to the Paris Métro were designed by the

Frenchman Hector Guimard (1867–1942) and symbolize the style in every aspect, the curvilinear 'whiplash' lines and the eclectic, exotic, natural references in its execution. In Vienna meanwhile, the Secessionists interpreted the style in a very different way that anticipated Modernism, particularly in architecture and the designed object. In graphics and the fine arts, however, the styles also departed from the exaggerated sinuous lines, but borrowed heavily from Symbolist motifs. One of the main influences for the Viennese style was the Glasgow Four, who participated at

the 1900 exhibition, introducing both the aspects of the 'spook school', through the MacDonald sisters, and the rectilinear forms of Charles Rennie Mackintosh (1868–1928), whose designs were key considerations in the formation of the *Wiener Werkstätte*. It was ironic, however, that it was those rectilinear forms, anticipating the Modernist aesthetic, that would instigate the downfall of the Art Nouveau style after 1905.

Although the style was widely interpreted in Europe, including areas not covered by this book, such as Prague and Helsinki, it did not catch on in England, despite its antecedents being there. It probably had much to do with the self-imposed isolationism of the country and the Continental excesses of the style that caused some to write disparaging remarks, most notably Crane who referred to it as a 'strange decorative disease'. Instead the style was readily adopted in parts of America, most notably in the graphic arts, and some aspects of the designs of Frank Lloyd Wright (1867–1956)

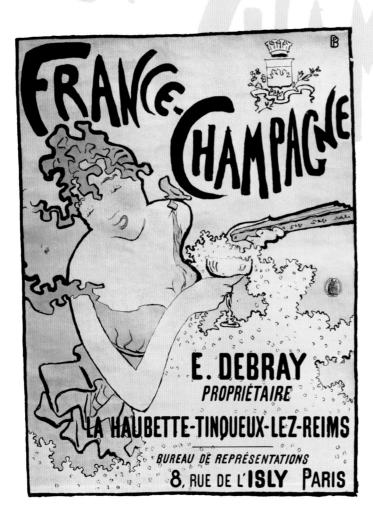

embrace the aesthetic too. Tiffany, who established his own glass-making premises in New York in 1893, played a crucial part in disseminating the style in the city. In fact, Art Nouveau is often still referred to in America as the 'Tiffany Style'.

This book concentrates on the fine and graphic arts in Art Nouveau and highlights the polarization of the style in terms of its contemporary consumer. For the designed object, the emphasis was on quality, craftsmanship and the use of expensive materials, making it an elitist item. In the graphic arts, however, the mass-produced poster was more affordable and therefore accessible to a wider public. It should be borne in mind that Art Nouveau was not a universal style, although there are similarities and themes that run through its aesthetic. It had different interpretations, some aligned to Symbolism and Romanticism, while others aspired to create a more progressive and modern style. The success of the 1900 Paris Exposition should be seen in terms of the former, an Art Nouveau movement whose excesses waned five years later. Its protagonists formed a collective known as *La Société des Artistes Décorateurs* and by 1907 were devising the next exposition to take place in 1915. In the event, the First World War interrupted these plans and it was not staged until 1925. This exhibition was the *Exposition Internationale des Arts Décoratifs et Industriels Modernes*. Its abbreviated terms, Art Deco and *Style Moderne*, are synonymous with the next generation, despite having their antecedents in Art Nouveau.

The more progressive aspects of Art Nouveau tended to be those interpreted in Germany and Vienna, seeking to use the 'new art' in a more comprehensive way, in the creation of the *Gesamtkunstwerk* that sought a fusion between fine art and design without denigrating either; and a progressive step towards better design in an industrial age. Hermann Muthesius (1861–1927) was perhaps the first to recognize the importance of the Arts and Crafts practitioners in Britain as the pioneers of modern design, writing a number of articles in *Dekorative Kunst*. He was also the motivational force behind the *Deutscher Werkbund*, a collaborative charged with improving design standard in Germany that included several Art Nouveau practitioners such as Josef Hoffmann (1870–1956) and Richard Riemerschmid (1868–1957).

What both factions were aware of was the spirit of change in the air. Perhaps the Romantics sought closure on a century that had seen a number of bloody revolutions, while the progressives looked forward to the potential of a new century. Either way they all embraced the spirit of a movement known as Art Nouveau.

HENRI
MEUNIER

Art Nouveau

Section One

The Movement

An overview of the Art Nouveau style,
a design ethos that swept across
continental Europe and America from
the late nineteenth century.

Beginnings

The term Art Nouveau encompasses many artistic forms. It embraces fine art, graphic art, architecture and the decorative arts. It has been given different name-tags: *Stile Liberty*, Whiplash, the 'macaroni' or 'noodle' style, Morris Style, Glasgow Style, *Jugendstil*, Métro Style and many more. In line with the many name-tags, Art Nouveau spread itself across many countries. Artists, designers and architects associated with the movement worked in separate nations yet created a widespread fusion of avant-garde ideas to collectively create the Art Nouveau movement. It was not intentional. On researching names associated with Art Nouveau one finds it to be the visual style that produced significantly common traits in artworks. Many artists associated with it did not set out to identify their work as Art Nouveau, or with a movement, yet their works nevertheless form the basis of what we identify to be Art Nouveau. Undoubtedly, the influence of Japanese prints, available in Europe from the 1850s, particularly those created by the masterful Katsushika Hokusai (1760–1849), Kitagawa Utamaro (1753–1806) and Andō Hiroshige (1797–1858), increased the motivation of European artists, who were inspired to integrate elements of Japanese design into their work.

Japanese Inspiration

In Paris, from the 1850s, interest in Japanese art quickly spread through arts tutors and artists meeting in ateliers and art schools dotted around the city. The influence of Japanese line drawings

Jules Chéret
Poster for *Pantomimes Lumineuses,*
***Théâtre Optique de E. Reynaud*, 1892**
© Private Collection/DaTo Images/
The Bridgeman Art Library

MEDIUM: Lithograph

RELATED WORKS: Jules Chéret,
Poster for *Pastilles Poncelet*, 1896

Jules Chéret
Poster for *Quinquina Dubonnet*, 1895
© Private Collection/The Stapleton
Collection/The Bridgeman Art Library

MEDIUM: Lithograph

RELATED WORKS: Jules Chéret,
Poster for *Job, papier a cigarettes*, 1889

QUINQUINA
DUBONNET
APÉRITIF
dans tous les Cafés
Imprimerie CHAIX, (Ateliers Chéret) rue Bergère, 20, Paris

can be seen in some of the Impressionist paintings from the 1870s where there is a preference for two-dimensional depictions, which accentuate the flatness of the image and lack of perspective. Works of Realism were of less interest to the new regime of painters who were not inspired to conform to the rules of the Académie Française. The graphic artists were influenced by

Japanese prints, and they were copied by popular poster artists, such as Jules Chéret (1836–1932) and Henri de Toulouse-Lautrec (1864–1901). Chéret's poster for *Pantomimes Lumineuses, Théâtre Optique de E. Reynaud*, 1892 (*see* page 12), printed by Chaix in Paris in 1892, highlights the gaiety of the city's nightlife. So, too, does Toulouse-Lautrec's 1895 advertisement for *May Milton* (*see* left).

Parisian Overture

With such a complex and intrinsically beautiful 'new art', which stretched from Europe to America, where should one begin? The earliest strands, which formed the backbone of the movement, came to fruition in Paris, in the mid-1890s. In parts of Montmartre, the medieval streets of Paris had resisted the modernization of the city by Baron Georges-Eugène Haussmann (1809–91). He had created a new centre for Paris from 1852 to 1870. Along Boulevard Haussmann and other avenues, which incorporated new parks and café concerts, the modernization of the city was a visual representation of change. The wide leafy streets and new apartment blocks typified the 'new' Paris, where the *flaneur* sauntered along boulevards, embracing the new city life.

The Impressionists

Paintings by the Impressionists mirrored the modernity of city life: its winners and losers. Claude Monet (1840–1926) and Gustave Caillebotte (1848–94) are just two examples of many artists who

Henri de Toulouse-Lautrec
May Milton, 1895
© San Diego Museum of Art, USA/
Gift of the Baldwin M. Baldwin
Foundation/The Bridgeman Art Library

MEDIUM: Lithograph

RELATED WORKS: Henri de
Toulouse-Lautrec, Poster for *Reine
de Joie*, 1892

Henri de Toulouse-Lautrec
Paul Sescau photography studio, 1896
© San Diego Museum of Art, USA/Gift
of the Baldwin M. Baldwin Foundation/
The Bridgeman Art Library

MEDIUM: Lithograph

RELATED WORKS: Henri de
Toulouse-Lautrec, Poster for *La Chaîne
Simpson (bicycle chains)*, 1896

mirrored the city's changes in their impressions of the city. In Montmartre, strands of the old and new came together in the music halls and café life. The *flaneur* mixed with artists and dancers, singers and seamstresses, ballerinas and businessmen. The Impressionists' flirtation with Japanese illustration is highlighted in works by the American artist Mary Cassatt (1845–1926), living in Paris. Cassatt's *The Letter*, 1890–91, an etching with dry point and aquatint, is a fine example, which one could compare to the exquisite wood-block print *O'Sen Sweeping up Love Letters*, c. 1750, by the Japanese artist Suzuki Harunobu (1725–70), created 100 years before Cassatt was born.

Poster Advertisements

Graphic artists favoured flat, line-drawn images, printed in two to four colours to highlight modernity. Poster art was hugely popular and the most-used form of advertising in Paris. Street walls were colourfully pasted roof-high in promotional posters for plays and musicals, ballet and opera, solo performances and café concerts. Advertisements for holiday travel, especially by train to the Côte d'Azur, mixed in with promotion of drinks, fashion and food. Chéret's advertising poster for *Quinquina Dubonnet*, 1895 (*see* page 13), captured the artifice and fun of it all. A young woman clutching a bottle of Dubonnet in one hand and a glass in the other smiles and beckons to the voyeur looking at her in the street. Her manner is far from the rigid etiquette of the refined Parisian woman who rarely stepped out alone. One example, which shows how popular poster art was in Paris, is an advertisement for the *Paul Sescau photography studio*, 1896 (*see* page 15). Sescau shunned the modern medium of photography to advertise his studio; instead, a Toulouse-Lautrec line drawing promoted Sescau's profession.

Two Cats

The modernity of Art Nouveau is depicted in *Two Cats*, 1894 (*see* left), a colour lithograph poster for the *Exposition de l'oeuvre dessiné et peint de T.A. Steinlen*, designed by Théophile-Alexandre Steinlen (1859–1923), to promote his painting and design

Théophile-Alexandre Steinlen
Two Cats, **1894**
© Museum of Fine Arts, Boston, Massachusetts, USA/Bequest of W.G. Russell Allen/The Bridgeman Art Library

MEDIUM: Lithograph

RELATED WORKS: Théophile-Alexandre Steinlen, Poster for *La Bodinière, 18 rue St. Lazare, Exposition de l'oeuvre dessiné et peint de T.A. Steinlen*, 1894

Théophile-Alexandre Steinlen
Poster for *Compagnie Francaise des Chocolats et des Thés*, *c.* **1896–98**
© Bibliotheque des Arts Décoratifs, Paris, France/Archives Charmet/The Bridgeman Art Library

MEDIUM: Lithograph

RELATED WORKS:
Théophile-Alexandre Steinlen, Poster for *Lait pur stérilisé de la Vingeanne*, 1894–95

Alphonse Mucha
Poster for *Champagne Ruinart*
(detail), 1896
© Mucha Trust 2009

MEDIUM: Lithograph

RELATED WORKS: Alphonse Mucha,
Poster for *Universal and International*
Exhibition in St. Louis, 1904

Alphonse Mucha
Poster for *Lance Parfum*
***Rodo*, 1896**
© Mucha Trust 2009

MEDIUM: Lithograph

RELATED WORKS: Eugène Grasset,
Poster for *Encre L. Marquet, La Meilleure*
de Toutes les Encres, 1892

exhibition in Paris. The image was created in watercolour on paper without the final lettering. Two cats of different colours are depicted in a two-dimensional plane. The black cat, in profile, accentuates the outline drawing and lack of perspective. Steinlen embraced modernity and the new style. A similar effect is seen in a poster advertisement for *Compagnie Francaise des Chocolats et des Thés*, c. 1896–98 (*see* page 17), where a cat peers into the picture space, drawing the viewer in to see the refreshments. The colour, typeface and form were influenced by the poster art of Toulouse-Lautrec, particularly the flattened perspective.

Sarah Bernhardt and Alphonse Mucha

To this day, the artist Alphonse Mucha (1860–1939), a Czechoslovakian *émigré* who lived and worked in Paris at the close of the 1880s, is recognized for the stunning posters he created for the famed Parisian stage actress Sarah Bernhardt (1844–1923). Bernhardt by chance changed the fortunes of the artist's life in the last days of 1894 when she approved his innovative poster design to advertise her play *Gismonda* (*see* pages 88–89). In return, Mucha gave Bernhardt a new persona through a quickly drawn graphic-art poster to promote her play. The public adored

en Poudre Soluble

Alphonse Mucha
Poster for *Chocolat Idéal,* 1897
© Mucha Trust 2009

MEDIUM: Lithograph

RELATED WORKS: Henri Meunier,
Poster for *Pollet et Vittet, Chocolaterie de
Pepinster, c.* 1896

Alphonse Mucha
Poster for *Job* (detail), 1896
© Mucha Trust 2009

MEDIUM: Lithograph

RELATED WORKS: Jules Chéret,
Poster for *Job, papier a cigarettes,* 1889

Bernhardt and embraced the Art Nouveau style of Mucha's graphic-art posters. He never agreed that he was an Art Nouveau artist, but his remarkable use of the curling tendril form, associated with the evolution of Art Nouveau, combined with his energetic use of colour in flattened perspective, created a new poster format. It was long and narrow in shape, which accentuated Mucha's slim, younger depiction of the middle-aged Bernhardt. He styled her hair with long tresses nicknamed the 'macaroni' or 'noodle' style, and used arabesque lines to break up the flat picture space and accentuate her curves and femininity.

Mucha's Art Nouveau Style

Mucha's fortunes changed through his new art form. He shook off his image of penniless artist to become a graphic-art designer, hugely in demand. Advertisers vied to use his skills to promote their products. The poster being the favoured choice, Mucha created a series of designs, which could equally sell champagne or chocolate drinks, perfume or train travel. His work captured the spirit of *fin-de-siècle,*

Alphonse Mucha
Poster for *Moët & Chandon:*
Champagne White Star, **1899**
© Mucha Trust 2009

MEDIUM: Lithograph

RELATED WORKS: Pierre Bonnard,
Poster for *France-Champagne,* 1894

neatly overlapping the end of one century with the new. For champagne products, such as a poster for *Champagne Ruinart,* 1896 (*see* page 18), Mucha included a young and beautiful woman with wind-blown flowing hair accentuated by sinuous tendrils of tresses. Its remarkable length is used to fill the background space. Young, beautiful women with long or short 'macaroni' style hair became Mucha's trademark, and that of Art Nouveau. Mucha used the geometric forms of circle, square and oblong to create *Lance Parfum Rodo,* 1896 (*see* pages 18–19), an advertisement for a pipette perfume spray; each shape is accentuated and softened by the feminine clothing of the young woman, who demonstrates the pipette's use.

Jewellery and Shop Design

In a poster for *Chocolat Idéal,* 1897 (*see* pages 20–21), Mucha uses the sinuous wavy line, not to accentuate hair but to curl the steam, which rises slowly from three cups of hot-chocolate drink, prepared from soluble chocolate powder. The dramatic effect of geometric form, highlighted by organic plant shapes and curving lines, was truly a fusion of the geometric and organic forms of Art

Nouveau, and much imitated by other artists. However, it was Mucha's flirtatious young women, such as the girl in a deliciously decorative poster for *Moët and Chandon: White Star Champagne*, 1899 (*see* left), that attracted most attention to the new art form. In it a young woman, entwined in vine tendrils and flower stems, holds in her palm the fruits of the vine, perhaps a symbol of a vintage year to end the century. It is a reminder of Walter Crane's (1845–1915) illustration *Flora's Feast*, created 10 years earlier.

Mucha eventually tired of the never-ending demand for advertising posters but welcomed new opportunities. One such request, from a Parisian jeweller Georges Fouquet (1862–1957), led him to design a selection of Art Nouveau jewellery for the Paris International Exhibition in 1900. The resulting success encouraged Fouquet to choose Mucha to design his new jewellery shop in Paris in 1901. The remarkable exterior and decorative interior led one reviewer to comment that 'the creations of Art Nouveau require a new kind of framework … [Fouquet] has been brave enough to make it a reality'.

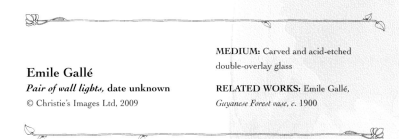

Emile Gallé
Pair of wall lights, **date unknown**
© Christie's Images Ltd, 2009

MEDIUM: Carved and acid-etched double-overlay glass

RELATED WORKS: Emile Gallé, *Guyanese Forest vase, c.* 1900

Etched in Glass: Emile Gallé

Two facets of Art Nouveau in France quickly defined the movement. One was the decorative work of graphic artists, the other was the decorative form of Art Nouveau in furnishings, furniture and glass. Two centres of the decorative arts developed in France. One was in the studio of the French woodworker and glass-maker Emile Gallé (1846–1904) in Nancy, where he produced imaginative pieces of furniture and glassware

that typify Art Nouveau. The other source originated from artists and designers commissioned by Siegfried Bing (1838–1905), a German *émigré* from Hamburg and a naturalized Frenchman, to sell wares in his decorative-arts shop in Paris. Primarily Gallé is known for dramatic pieces of glassware, produced in double layers of glass, which allowed separate colours and decoration to enrich the design. Gallé used a variety of organic shapes, many inspired by oriental design. A perfect example of popular glassware designed by Gallé for the contemporary market is a *Pair of wall lights* (*see* page 23), in carved and etched double-overlay glass, decorated with natural plant forms. The burnished leaves and rich-red flower heads are signature style. The addition of Gallé's own signature ensured the authenticity of the pieces and destined them to be collectors' items. Gallé's innovative glassware proactively embraced the organic form of Art Nouveau.

L'Art Nouveau Bing

In 1896, six years on from the successful opening of the English Liberty store in Paris, a new shop, much smaller in size, called L'Art Nouveau, opened to sell furniture, furnishings and interior decorative art. It was owned by Siegfried Bing. On the premises he brought together a significant group of European designers and artists and set up his own studio to make luxury objects for his wealthy middle-class clientele. Bing had taken an interest in Japanese pottery from a visit to the country in 1875, and following his visit he imported pottery and decorative art from Japan. His first shop opened at 19 rue de Chauchat, Paris. To either side of the entrance were vast metal sculptures of decorative sunflowers. The sign advertised *'Entrée des Galeries d'Art Japonais'*. Bing found the imported pottery wrapped in paper covered in line drawings, which inspired him and his artistic friends.

French School
Poster for *Byrrh, Tonique Hygienique, c.* 1900
© Private Collection/Patrice Cartier/
The Bridgeman Art Library

MEDIUM: Engraving

RELATED WORKS: Frederic Leighton
(1830–96), *Flaming June*, 1895

La Maison Moderne

From his emporium Bing pushed forward an interest in everything Japanese. The style varied from the thin wavy line, favoured by artists, to a purer geometric form for decorative arts and architecture. However, this was not Europe's first exposure to Japanese design. Japan had opened its shores to trade with the United States of America with the arrival of Commodore Matthew C. Perry in 1854, and trade soon expanded to European countries. From Bing's luxury end of the new market, and Liberty's new venture, other stores followed on to sell the 'Orient' to the public. One was La Maison Moderne, which opened in Paris in 1899 and was owned by the German writer, art critic and entrepreneur, Julius Meier-Graefe (1867–1935). He was a friend of Bing's and took a keen interest in European artists' interpretations and incorporation of Japanese art forms. 'Taste' was moving away from Orientalism, a European fusion of East meets West, which combined Chinese and Japanese art forms to suit European homes, but the Japanese-inspired Art Nouveau spread to mass appreciation by the turn of the century, creating an omnipresent appetite for cheap products in the new style. This was lost on Bing who by 1900 had turned his attention towards French eighteenth-century design, a new vogue for the avant-garde collector.

Graphic Artists in Demand

The fortunate timing of Mucha's meeting with Sarah Bernhardt in Paris in 1894 focused attention on graphic poster art as the preferred medium to advertise goods. Everything, from the craze for bicycling, to chocolate drinks and the printing press, found graphic artists willing to transform a plain product into a must-have item. The formula for an Art Nouveau image tended to include one or two young women wearing seductive clothing, with beautiful hair, preferably in the 'macaroni' style popularized by Mucha. A decorative background, a profusion of flowers and a variation of typeface completed the style. *Byrrh, Tonique Hygienique, c.* 1900 (*see* right) (French School), has the ingredients. The printing press for posters and artwork was part of the modern hub of city life in Paris. Printers and publishers looked at all forms of printing to sell products, including personal visiting cards, theatrical posters, limited edition books and prints, and limited edition posters, and the popular *panneaux décoratifs* series of lithographs for collectors. The result meant an increasing amount of work for illustrators and graphic poster artists as Paris continued to draw aspiring artists to the city. Many lived frugally whilst hoping for recognition. Their dream was to create masterpieces in oils, yet the reality was a lucky break to obtain work as a graphic artist. However, in an unusual twist on arts tradition, in the last years of the nineteenth century the fortunes and reputation of many graphic artists from French-born Toulouse-Lautrec to *émigré* Mucha soared. Graphic poster art was highly prized with some editions, particularly those inspired by Art Nouveau, becoming collectors' items.

Inspired Colourists

Paul Emile Berthon (1872–1909)
is perhaps typical of the successful
graphic artist in Paris at the end of the
nineteenth century. Berthon studied
painting in Villefranche, coming to live
in Paris in 1893. He enrolled, as many
artists did, at a school of painting.
Berthon chose the École Normale
d'Enseignement de Dessin. He
received tuition from Luc-Oliver
Merson (1846–1920) in painting and
from Eugène Grasset (1845–1917)
in decorative art. Grasset had an astounding impact on Berthon's
work. It is visible in the highly decorative and colourful *Two Girls
with a Printing Press*, c. 1896 (*see* above and far left). Berthon became
known as one of the foremost interpreters of Art Nouveau. He is
noted for his series of *panneaux décoratifs*, intended as collectors'
items without typeface or advertising. Progressing from Grasset's
initial inspiration, Berthon's art is recognized for its interpretation of
Japanese woodcuts and interest in French medieval art, combined
to create a synthesis of Art Nouveau iconography. Another success
was the Parisian-born artist, Maurice Réalier-Dumas (1860–1928),
who studied under Jean-Léon Gérôme (1824–1904) at the École
des Beaux-Arts. His style fits the Art Nouveau era and yet his
graphic-art compositions, such as *Champagne by Jules Mumm et
Co., Reims*, 1895 (*see* left), created at the same time Bing opened
his Art Nouveau shop in Paris, invoke a refined expression of
Art Nouveau. It is closer to the graphic art of the Art Deco style,
which gained momentum in the early twentieth century.

Paul Berthon
Two Girls with a Printing Press, c. 1896
© Royal Albert Memorial Museum, Exeter,
Devon, UK/The Bridgeman Art Library

MEDIUM: unknown

RELATED WORKS: Paul Berthon,
Femme de Profil (Woman in Profile), 1898

Maurice Réalier-Dumas
Poster for *Champagne by Jules
Mumm et Co., Reims*, **1895**
© Bibliotheque des Arts Décoratifs, Paris, France/
Archives Charmet/The Bridgeman Art Library

MEDIUM: Lithograph

RELATED WORKS: Alphonse Mucha,
Menu for *Moët & Chandon*, 1899

28

Eugène Grasset

Grasset was a masterful mediator in graphic art and decorative design. He was born in Switzerland but moved to Paris in 1871 where he mastered the design intricacies of ceramics, jewellery, furniture and tapestries. His innovative jewellery and very popular textiles sold in Magasin du Printemps in Paris. However, by 1877 he turned towards graphic design where his gift for creating the extraordinary allowed him to design a variety of graphic works including poster advertisements and book illustrations. Capturing the carefree style of bike riding, Grasset's design for an advertisement for *Georges Richard Cycles and Automobiles*, c. 1897 (*see* right) used natural colours: earthy browns and shades of green contrast the amber and rust dress of a female cyclist. In the poster the bike owner contemplates the pleasures of the countryside through the symbol of one of the flower heads, enlarged and held in the young woman's hand. The clarity of the storyline and underlying message – cycling and motor travel equal fresh air and freedom – is mediated through an organic interpretation of the Art Nouveau form.

Hector Guimard's Paris

At the time of the opening of Bing's Art Nouveau shop in Paris, a young French designer, Hector Guimard (1867–1942), was building the outrageously different *Castel Béranger* (*see* page 30) in Paris, for his client Madame Fournier. Guimard had studied at the École des Arts Décoratifs and at the École Nationale des Beaux-Arts in Paris, taking an interest in the theoretical work of Eugène Emmanuel Viollet-le-Duc (1814–79). Guimard graduated in 1889 and at the time of the *Castel Béranger* commission he was

Eugène Grasset
Poster for *Georges Richard Cycles and Automobiles*, c. 1897
© Deutsches Historisches Museum, Berlin, Germany/© DHM Indra Desnica/The Bridgeman Art Library

MEDIUM: Lithograph

RELATED WORKS: Alphonse Mucha, Poster for *Waverley Cycles*, 1897

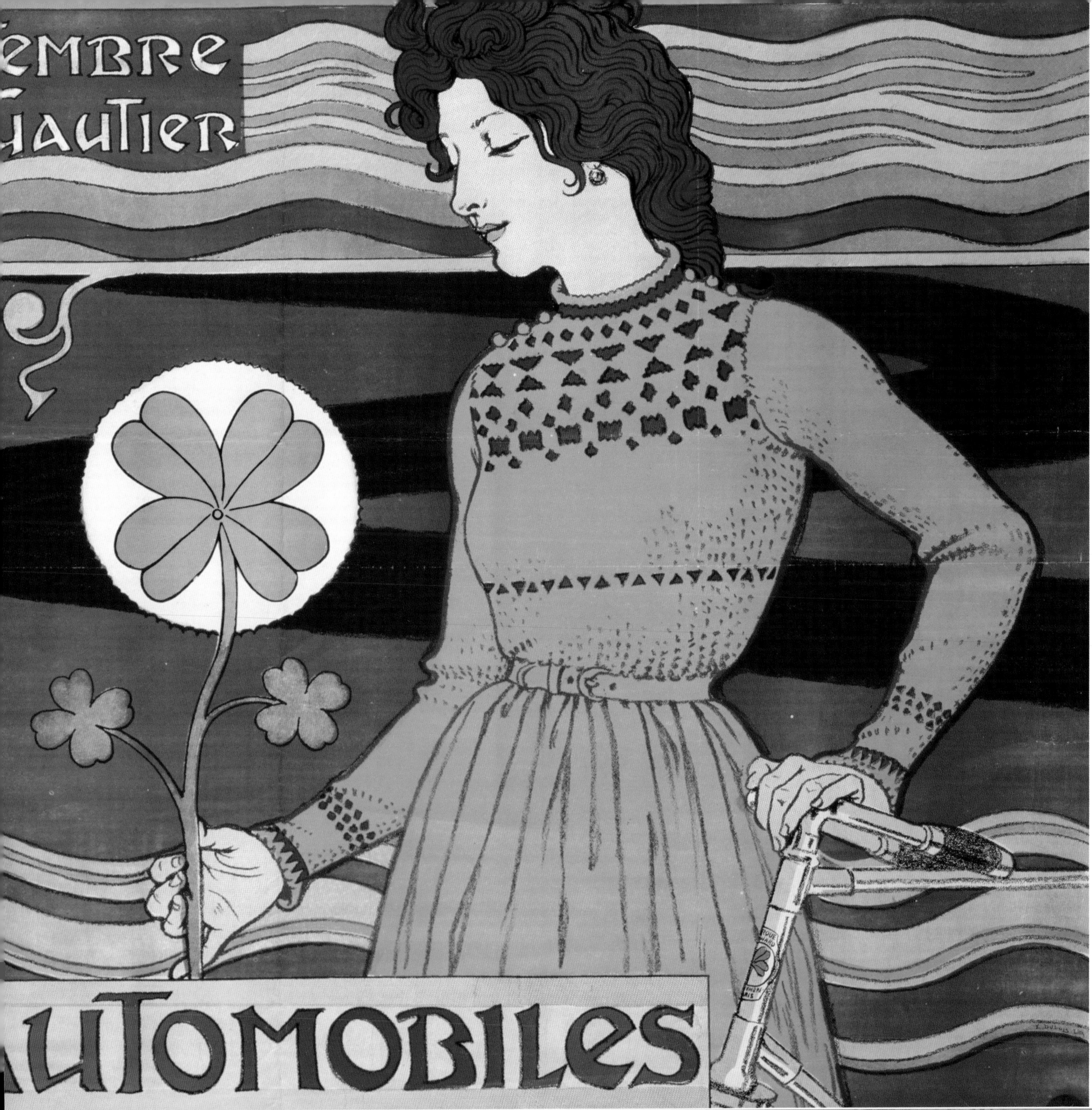
EMBRE
AUTIER
UTOMOBILES

still in his twenties. His organic designs have much in common with the fantasy designs and magical creations of the Spanish architect Antoni Gaudí (1852–1926) and the early houses of Henry van de Velde (1863–1957) in Belgium, which Guimard visited. All are definitions of Art Nouveau and each designer has contributed to the success of the movement.

The Metropolitan Line

In Guimard's work one can identify historic symbolism wrapped up in new art forms through the bold use of modern materials in architecture and interior design. A dramatic piece of Art Nouveau was constructed in Paris from 1898 to 1901 by Guimard. His imaginative designs for the public entrances to the Metropolitan line of the Paris underground used iron and glass with metallic twists of his signature plant motifs. One can identify a resemblance to ironwork structures designed by Viollet-le-Duc. Each of the entrances is different, yet the design motif is carried to all, in the use of dark-green cast-iron supports and prefabricated and interchangeable sections of glass and ironwork. The *Porte Dauphine entrance to the Métro*, 1898–1901 (*see* below), is clearly signposted with a frosted-glass roof, splayed out over

the entrance. Keeping it in place are organic plant forms of intertwined vines of metalwork, twisted around each other and rising up, either side of the entrance, to meet high up in the centre as support for the glass roof. Guimard's embrace of Art Nouveau and his use in the design for the Métro entrances are viewed now as iconic symbols of the *fin-de-siècle* era.

Hector Guimard
Entrance to Castel Béranger,
Paris, 1894–98
© Estate of Hector Guimard/Bibliotheque
des Arts Décoratifs, Paris, France/Archives
Charmet/The Bridgeman Art Library

MEDIUM: unknown

RELATED WORKS: Antoni Gaudí,
Park Güell, Barcelona, 1900–14

Hector Guimard
Porte Dauphine entrance to the
Métro, Paris, 1898–1901
© Estate of Hector Guimard/Private
Collection/Archives Charmet/
The Bridgeman Art Library

MEDIUM: Architecture (metalwork)

RELATED WORKS: Hector Guimard,
Jassedé Apartment Building, Paris, 1903–05

Tiffany Studios
Blue Wisteria table lamp, c. 1908
© Christie's Images Ltd, 2009

MEDIUM: Leaded glass and bronze

RELATED WORKS: Louis Comfort
Tiffany, *Bronze and glass table lamp, c. 1900*

Art Nouveau: In Belgium

The Belgian contribution to the formation of an Art Nouveau
movement is drawn from Belgium's artist colonies, societies
and salons, and the Belgian writers, artists and designers who
contributed to the arts journals that flourished in Europe in
the mid-to-late nineteenth century. Today two names primarily
dominate the new architecture and decorative art of the period.
Both were young men in the 1880s: Victor Horta (1861–1947)
and van de Velde. In addition to individual accomplishments
in Belgium, an artists' collective *Les Vingt* (also known as *Les
XX*) was formed in 1884. It was created to allow freedom of
expression in art, a reaction to the formality of the official Salon.
The artistic production of *Les Vingt* was admirably promoted
in *L'Art Moderne*, an arts and literary journal that was initiated
in 1881 by a lawyer, writer and art critic, Octave Maus
(1856–1919). The profusion of talents in Belgian architecture,
decorative arts, painting and graphic art, published in Belgium's
avant-garde arts journal, ensured a pan-European audience for
the country's artists. The plan was to not only create new forms
of design, but also to tap into the commercial ventures available
to innovative designers. For example, Tiffany Studios' *Blue
Wisteria table lamp, c. 1908 (see right)*, created in leaded glass and
bronze, was made in a limited edition of 2,000, thus ensuring its
status as a global collector's item. If it worked for American
importers, perhaps it could work for Belgian exporters too.

Les Vingt

The group formed in rebellion of the formal academy of painting,
the Salon. Prior to the formation of *Les Vingt*, many of its members,
who had broken away from the Salon, had joined a new Belgian
group *Essor* but found its strict set of rules too demanding. The
mission of *Les Vingt* was to create a collective group of artists,

free to explore their own creativity without regulation and control. Founders included the talented Belgian artists, Théo van Rysselberghe (1862–1926) and James Ensor (1860–1949), and later other nationalities, including the Dutchman Jan Toorop (1858–1928). The 20 were created from nine founder members and 11 invited members. The group accepted many other artists from different countries including Britain, Holland, France and Spain, which pushed numbers beyond the initial 20. However, it was the original founding members, along with secretary Maus, who initiated organization of the group, the selection of invited members and overseas members and the promotion of its society.

L'Art Moderne (1881–1914)

One only has to study the 1880s in Belgium to see how art and literature went hand-in-hand to promote Belgian artists, poets, writers and designers as a collective force of creativity. The Belgian lawyer, writer and art critic Maus was integral to the formation of ideas and collective ideology of the *Les Vingt*. He acted as secretary and worked closely with *Les Vingt*, his friends and colleagues, to set up art exhibitions to promote their work. They would regularly feature in Maus's weekly arts journal *L'Art Moderne*, which he founded in 1881 with writer Edmond Picard (1836–24), Victor Arnould (1838–93) and Eugène Robert (1831–1912). The Belgian poet Emile Verhaeren (1855–1916) was a contributor, illustrating the collective interest in art and literature. The first issue was printed on 6 March 1881. The magazine was published every Sunday until 9 August 1914, when the onset of war in Europe halted its production. The co-ordinators of the magazine chose to print featured articles unsigned until 1898, perhaps in keeping with a collective contribution of ideas. In 1893 Maus was instrumental in the decision to disband *Les Vingt*. In 1894 it was reformed as *La Libre Esthétique* and once again promoted in *L'Art Moderne*.

Henri Privat-Livemont
Poster for *Robette Absinthe*
(detail), 1896
© Private Collection/The Stapleton
Collection/The Bridgeman Art Library

MEDIUM: Lithograph

RELATED WORKS: Alphonse Mucha,
Poster for *Vin des Incas*, 1899

Victor Horta

It is perhaps Horta's extraordinary design for the house of Professor Tassel at 12 rue de Turin (now 6 rue Paul Emil Janson) in Brussels that defines the innovative contribution of Belgian Art Nouveau. *Tassel House*, designed and built from 1893 to 1897, used historical reference to Classical architecture on the exterior, reworked by Horta's use of industrial materials, particularly cast and wrought ironwork. Horta's ingenious delivery of both abstract and organic plant forms combined to create an overwhelmingly beautiful interior. The interior walls and floor of the entrance hall were decorated in arabesque coils of wispy plant tendrils, echoed on the cast-iron supporting columns and the wrought-iron staircase.

Henry van de Velde

In 1880 van de Velde was studying painting in his home town of Antwerp but by 1884 he was living in Paris. The French capital was the heart of the art world and young artists from Europe and America aspired to live, work and become successful in Paris. However, van de Velde did not stay in Paris permanently. Five years later in 1889, he found work at the Belgian arts journal *L'Art Moderne*. Three years on, in 1892, he made the decision to give up painting, in order to concentrate on decorative and applied art. He planned to create furniture to complement the interiors of the houses he designed, combining historicism with elements of modern living. One can see from examples of his work where the dynamism of the new art form, Art Nouveau, derived. Van de Velde fused abstract form with asymmetrical design, particularly in organic plant forms, mixing new materials with old, to create a unique form of architecture and decorative design. A house and interior that van de Velde designed for himself at Uccle, Brussels in 1895 was visited by French promoters of Art Nouveau, Bing and Meier-Graefe. The visit resulted in Bing commissioning van de Velde to create four room settings to exhibit at his Art Nouveau shop in Paris. One can see from this liaison how new forms of Art Nouveau travelled and the interest it inspired. In Germany the popularity of his decorative art, particularly furniture, led him to form a

company, Van de Velde GmbH, in Berlin in 1898. His creative versatility covered many fields of art including typography, book illustration and poster design. His graphic art in the poster for *Tropon*, *c.* 1898 (*see* page 128) was designed for a food manufacturer. The design combined linearity with a triple form of loosely coiled whiplash forms and the result was a pleasing abstract of colour, line and form, similar in composition to the ironwork entrance gate of *Castel Béranger* (*see* page 30), in Paris, designed by Guimard between 1894 and 1898.

Belgian Artists

One of the most-prolific graphic artists in Belgium was the little-known Henri Privat-Livemont (1861–1936), whose name came to prominence in Belgium in the 1890s. Livemont had established himself as a painter when by chance he won a prize for a poster design at an art exhibition. His prize encouraged him to learn the art of lithography. It created a wealth of work, mainly advertising posters. His *La Belle Époque* style and Art Nouveau graphics were extremely popular with advertisers, publicists and consumers. For poster work Livemont preferred to include semi-naked young women. He created his posters at a time when Mucha was enjoying similar success in Paris. Livemont had trained in Paris. His poster for *Robette Absinthe*, 1896 (*see* page 32), is a signature style: a young girl, in three-quarter profile, is naked under a transparent swathe of material. Her head, in profile, is framed in a halo of light. She delicately holds a tall glass of absinthe up to the light. The background is decorated with a mass of abstract organic shapes: pure Art Nouveau. The close relationship between Paris and Brussels, through its artists and graphic art meant that not all Belgian advertisers looked to their own artists to create promotional publicity. A colour lithograph advertising a Brussels company *PD Corsets* (*see* left) is the work of a French school of graphic art.

The 'Whiplash' Line

The lithographer, etcher and Symbolist painter Henri Georges Jean Isadore Meunier (1873–1922) was born into an artistic family in Ixelles, Brabant. His father Jean-Baptiste Meunier (1821–1900) was an etcher and an uncle was the noted French sculptor and painter Constantin Meunier (1831–1905), whose sculptures in the Art Nouveau style were regularly promoted at *Les Vingt* exhibitions. Henri Meunier would follow the family tradition. *Rajah, c.* 1897 (*see* pages 124–25), an advertisement for coffee, contains the sinuous curves of Art Nouveau form, which depict the steam rising from the coffee cup. The work was hailed as a masterpiece and sold as part of *Les Maîtres de l'Affiche* series, by subscription to collectors. Meunier used the same technique for a postcard of a *Woman with Binoculars, c.* 1900 (*see* right). The Art Nouveau 'whiplash' is visible in the back fastening of the woman's dress; she has a floral decoration in her neatly coiffed hair, and yet it is the contrast of feminine form against a four-colour geometric background that draws the viewer into the picture plane. The work is reminiscent of the Impressionist paintings a few decades earlier, yet the geometric lines combined with softer, curving forms show it to be Art Nouveau in its synthesis of Japanese design.

Jugendstil

Various strands of interest in Art Nouveau, or *Jugendstil* as it was called in Germany, came together in the artist communes and schools of art and design formed towards the end of the nineteenth century, most importantly in schools of applied and decorative art. *Jugendstil* flourished in Berlin and Darmstadt, Munich and Dresden. Its popularity was further promoted through the arts journal *Jugend*, loosely translated as 'youth', which aimed to promote the latest literature, art and decorative art. It was a weekly arts publication that began in 1896 (and published until 1940), with a mantra to highlight the latest ideas without preference for any particular trend or movement. The *Jugend* initial print run was for 30,000, peaking at 200,000.

HENRI
MEUNIER

The intense interest and preference for Art Nouveau in drawing, painting and decorative design curtailed the promotion of other forms. A cover illustration of the 4 September 1897 issue gives an idea of the style direction. Entitled *Lovers on a Bench* (*see* below),

two lovers, fashionably dressed, meet to kiss and talk. The cover symbolizes the magazine title, a youthful style and a youthful outlook towards the future. The design is by Otto Eckmann (1865–1902). At the same time a subscription-only magazine journal *Pan*, circulated to about 500 subscribers from 1895. The editorial content was controlled by the German art critic Meier-Graefe. Other magazines, centred in different cities, brought the design style of the Art Nouveau movement to the arts communities and to the attention of the public.

Berlin Secession

The Berlin *Secession* was formed in 1898, by 65 artists eager to promote the progressive art. Its members were predominantly those who shunned, or were shunned by, the official academy system. Max Liebermann (1847–1935) was president. Two cousins, Bruno Cassirer (1871–1941) and his cousin Paul Cassirer (1871–1926), well known in arts circles and owners of a Berlin art gallery and a publishing house, promoted the avant-garde artists. The *Secession* was held twice a year. It followed earlier group formations, notably in Munich in 1892. The youth of Germany were interested in new art forms and the Berlin *Secession*, an exposition of new art and decorative design, attracted a healthy audience. The poster for the 1900

Otto Eckmann
Lovers on a Bench, **cover illustration for** *Jugend,* **1897**
© Bibliotheque des Arts Décoratifs, Paris, France/Archives Charmet/ The Bridgeman Art Library

MEDIUM: Lithograph

RELATED WORKS: Pierre-Auguste Renoir (1841–1919), *Lovers,* 1875

German School
Poster for *the Berlin Secession Exhibition,* **1900**
© Private Collection/Barbara Singer/ The Bridgeman Art Library

MEDIUM: Lithograph

RELATED WORKS: Joseph Maria Olbrich, Poster for *Second Vienna Secession Exhibition,* 1898

exhibition (*see* page 37), possibly designed by the Berlin Secessionists, features key symbols of the artist and the era: a young woman holds an artist's paintbrushes and palette in her left hand and a flame-lit torch in her right. The Berlin *Secession* helped many artists who did not fit the mainstream art and design ethos, particularly the restrictive form of 'true art' promoted by Kaiser Wilhelm II (1859–1941). However, by 1910, the *Secession* had run its course; too many voices with disparate ideas failed to make the unit work. Notably successful artists who began at the Berlin *Secession* include Lovis Corinth (1858–1925) and Walter Leistikow (1865–1908).

Peter Behrens

One of the most important figures in the history of German *Jugendstil* (Art Nouveau) was the German architect and artist Peter Behrens (1868–1940). He was instrumental in the teaching and promotion of applied and decorative arts and crafts. Behrens is noted for the simplicity and functionality of his designs: whether a building, a light fixture, or the clean lines and pared-back decoration of a porcelain *Cup and saucer*, 1901 (*see* right). Behrens was born in Hamburg in 1869. He studied painting at the Karlsruhe School of Art in the city before continuing in Düsseldorf under Ferdinand Brütt (1849–1936). Behrens was one of the founding members of the Munich *Secession* in 1893 and the *Freie Vereinigung Münchener Kunstler* (Independent Association of Munich Artists), with Eckmann.

The Kiss, 1898

One of Behrens' best-known Art Nouveau works is a richly coloured woodcut called *The Kiss*, 1898 (*see* left), printed in green and rust, and light, medium and dark brown, on thin laid paper. In it Behrens illustrates two faces in profile, meeting to kiss. The picture plane is filled with curving shapes and voluptuous swirling cascades of hair, which frame

Walter Thor
Poster for *Peugeot Bicycles*, c. 1905–10
© Private Collection/DaTo Images/
The Bridgeman Art Library

MEDIUM: Lithograph

RELATED WORKS:
Henri de Toulouse-Lautrec, Poster for
La Chaine Simpson (bicycle chains), 1896

Peter Behrens
Cup and saucer, 1901
Courtesy of Private Collection/Photo
© Christie's Images/The Bridgeman
Art Library/© DACS 2009

MEDIUM: Porcelain

RELATED WORKS: Rosenthal Porcelain
Company, *Porcelain cup and saucer, c. 1902*

the faces. It typifies *fin-de-siècle* German art. Behrens' woodcut was published in *Pan*, volume 4, issue no.2, 1898. He was part of the group associated with the art and literary journal, a leading periodical for German art. During the 1890s, Behrens regularly exhibited his paintings but by the end of the 1890s he had turned

Joseph Maria Olbrich
Poster for *Secession Exhibition*
of Austrian Artists, **1898**
© Private Collection/The Bridgeman
Art Library

MEDIUM: Lithograph

RELATED WORKS: Otto Wagner
(1841–1918), *Academy of Fine Arts, Vienna*
(design for the Hall of Honour), 1898

Koloman Moser
Poster for *Frommes Calendar,* **1902**
© Private Collection/The Bridgeman
Art Library

MEDIUM: Lithograph

RELATED WORKS: Alphonse Mucha,
Poster for *Cours Mucha,* 1897

to graphic and applied arts. His design work included furniture
and jewellery, glass and porcelain. Later he was appointed by
Ernst-Ludwig, Grand Duke of Hesse Darmstadt (1868–1937),
to lead the *Kunstler-Kolonie* in Darmstadt. Other German artists,
for example Walter Thor (1870–1929), continued to produce
popular poster art for advertising and promotion, such as *Peugeot
Bicycles, c.* 1905–10 (*see* page 38), a quite different form of Art
Nouveau, yet still defined by the influence of Japanese prints,
seen in the use of fluent outlines and large areas of flat colour.

Wiener Secession

In Austria, in Vienna, a group of like-minded, progressive
artists and designers, writers and architects got together to form
the *Wiener Secession* (Vienna *Secession*) on 3 April 1897. The plan
was to work together to produce a total work of art; in German
it is called *Gesamtkunstwerk*. Notable members of the group
included the writer Hermann Bahr (1863–1934), the furniture
designer Josef Hoffmann (1870–1956) and the artist Gustav
Klimt (1862–1918). The motto carved above the entrance to the
Secession building is 'to every age its art and to art its freedom'.

Architecture and Jugendstil

A different form of *Jugendstil* was evident in Austrian
architecture. One only has to look at the *Villa Steiner*, 1910, by
Adolf Loos (1870–1933) to see Austrian vernacular architecture
combined with an asymmetrical free plan, which is seen as a
prototype for the Modern movement. The plan for the *Post Office
Savings Bank* in Vienna, 1904–12, designed by Otto Wagner
(1841–1918) moved towards Modernism in its lack of applied

ornament, floral or organic shapes. A lack of ornamentation was noticeable, too, in furniture design by Hoffmann. In the poster art of Joseph Maria Olbrich (1867–1908), for example *Secession*, 1898 (*see* page 40), advertising the *Secession* exhibition of Austrian Artists, Olbrich combined vestiges of *Jugendstil* with a sharp typeface that mirrored the purity of the *Secession* building it portrayed. The group wanted to move away from historicism, which allowed the building to be loosely based on a free plan. Only the gold of the 'cabbage cap' roof retained a little of the recognizable *Jugendstil*.

Art and Jugendstil

In the poster for *Frommes Kalendar*, 1902 (*see* page 41), by Koloman Moser (1868–1918), there is the recognizable form of Japanese-inspired line drawing. A young woman in profile looks left. Her hair flows dramatically across the picture plane and is tied at the back with a floral posy. The image is Art Nouveau. Did the art of the Vienna *Secession* group differ from the architecture and furniture design? One glance at the work of Klimt, a member of the *Secession* group and its first president, finds the spirit of *Jugendstil*. Klimt's cover page of *Ver Sacrum*, 1898 (*see* left) – the journal of the Viennese *Secession* published from January 1898 to October 1903 – would point to a use of historicism. He depicts the Greek goddess Athena, shield in hand, standing in profile looking to the left; in the background above her a battle between Theseus and the Minotaur is taking place. The form of the lithograph is inspired by Japanese prints; its content is a combination of Symbolism and Art Nouveau.

Femme Fatales

Klimt is recognized as the pre-eminent expression of Art Nouveau. His highly decorative paintings of women are superb examples of his use of Japanese print design and application of bold colour. His 'women' are often beautiful; some pose erotically; many are near naked. *Judith*, 1901 (*see* page 44), is Klimt's version of the brave Jewish widow who, through seduction, decapitates Holofernes, an Assyrian chieftain who is about to invade her city of Bethulia. The lithe body and nudity of 'Judith' caused a stir when the painting was exhibited. Although Klimt takes the Old Testament story as the basis of his work, the seductive manner of the model left critics uneasy.

Gustav Klimt
Cover of *Ver Sacrum*, 1898
© Wien Museum Karlsplatz, Vienna,
Austria/The Bridgeman Art Library

MEDIUM: Lithograph

RELATED WORKS: Gustav Klimt,
Initial "D" Drawing, 1898

Emile Gallé
Lamp, c. 1900
© The Art Archive/Private
Collection/Dagli Orti

MEDIUM: Double-layered glass

RELATED WORKS: Muller Frères
(1895–1933), *Cameo table lamp, c.* 1905–06

In contrast, the picture plane for *The Three Ages of Women*, 1905 (*see* far right), was divided into three sections. In the central section Klimt depicted two nude women: one a young woman with flowing golden hair, who holds an infant girl in her arms and rests her cheek on its head; and close by, in profile facing right, is an older woman with head hanging down. The paunch belly of the older woman contrasts with the slim figure of the young one.

Historicism

Klimt is known to have drawn on a vast variety of sources. In his paintings one can find expressions of Egyptian and Minoan art; the influence of Classical Greece and Near-East Byzantium; medieval painting and inspiration from individual artists and art mediums, such as the woodcuts of the German Northern-Renaissance painter and engraver, Albrecht Dürer (1471–1528). The nature of Klimt's decorative art leaves the viewer searching for sources. This is by definition the art of *fin-de-siècle* Art Nouveau, a fusion of historicism with the application of colour and form. *Fulfilment*, from the *Stoclet Frieze*, *c.* 1905–09 (*see* page 46), in tempera and watercolour is a good example. Historicism was evident too in many decorative pieces of this period. In the *Lamp*, *c.* 1900 (*see* page 43), designed by Gallé, the symbolism of

Gustav Klimt
Judith, 1901
© Österreichische Galerie Belvedere,
Vienna, Austria/The Bridgeman Art Library

MEDIUM: Oil on canvas

RELATED WORKS: Gustav Klimt,
Fritza Riedler, 1906

Gustav Klimt
The Three Ages of Woman, 1905
© Galleria Nazionale d'Arte Moderna,
Rome, Italy/Alinari/The Bridgeman
Art Library

MEDIUM: Oil on canvas

RELATED WORKS: Alphonse Mucha,
Folio from *Ilsée, Princesse de Tripoli*, 1987

the Orient is connoted by the green and gold 'coolie' hat glass shade, and denoted by the cluster of buildings etched on the globe of the lamp base. A stunning *Tea service, c.* 1905 (*see* below), in silver-gilt by Hoffmann, uses the Classical symbol of welcome, the pineapple, as lid holders. The body of the teapot, hot-water pot, sugar bowl and milk jug may have taken inspiration from Eastern architecture. It is the new look that Hoffmann had created that inspired *Jugendstil*, and which Hoffmann himself expressed so well in his decorative art.

Gustav Klimt
Fulfilment, **from the** *Stoclet Frieze*
(detail), *c.* **1905–09**
© MAK (Austrian Museum of Applied Arts), Vienna, Austria/The Bridgeman Art Library

MEDIUM: Tempera and watercolour

RELATED WORKS: Gustav Klimt, *Danae,* 1907–08

Josef Hoffmann
Tea service, c. 1905
© Estate of Josef Hoffmann/Lucie Rie, London, UK/The Bridgeman Art Library

MEDIUM: Silver-gilt

RELATED WORKS: Christopher Dresser (1834–1904), *Electroplate and porcelain teapot* (made by Hurkin & Heath), 1875

Gustav Klimt
Die Hoffnung II (Hope II)
(detail), 1907–08
© Fischer Fine Art Ltd, London, UK/
The Bridgeman Art Library

MEDIUM: Oil on canvas

RELATED WORKS: Gustav Klimt, *Tragedy*
(Study for the Allegory
of Tragedy), 1879

Gustav Klimt
Judith II (Salome) **(detail), 1909**
© Museo d'Arte Moderna, Venice,
Italy/ Cameraphoto Arte Venezia/
The Bridgeman Art Library

MEDIUM: Oil on canvas

RELATED WORKS: Fernand Khnopff
(1858–1921), *Stéphane Mallarmé's Poetry*
(Listening to Flowers), 1892

From Secession to Werkstätte

By 1903 members of the original Vienna *Secession*, including
Hoffmann, Moser, Olbrich and Wagner, alongside others
artists and artisans in the group, officially registered the *Wiener*
Werkstätte. By 1905 Klimt had left the Vienna *Secession*, stepping
down as president. He and his colleagues had achieved much
and made Vienna a pivotal city for progressive art, architecture
and design. After this date Klimt produced *Die Hoffnung II (Hope*
II), 1907–08 (*see* left), and *Judith II (Salome)*, 1909 (*see* right).
In the latter, the narrow frame and flat space of the picture
plane draw attention to the female figure moving from right
to left. She is semi-naked and the open folds of her dress reveal
her upper body. The head of John the Baptist, eyes closed,
is placed to the bottom right. Klimt used dramatically dark
colours to highlight the paleness of Salome's skin and the
tense, clutching movement of her claw-like hands.

Historicism versus Modernity

The artists of Italy are not known to have made any avant-
garde contribution to the Art Nouveau movement. However,
a poster produced in 1895, one of many designed by the
Roman artist Giovanni Maria Mataloni (1869–1944) showed
an Italian interpretation of Art Nouveau. Mataloni trained as a
lithographer for four years. In the colour lithograph *Incandescent*
Gas Lamps, 1895 (*see* page 50), he included a giant sunflower,
which curled and coiled its stalks and tendrils around the
poster's inner edge. The modernity of the gas lamp shone light
in a halo from the head of a half-naked kneeling girl. The lamp
revealed the modernity of the design, which used Art Nouveau

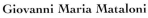

Giovanni Maria Mataloni
Poster for *Incandescent Gas Lamps*, 1895
© Estate of Giovanni Maria Mataloni/
Private Collection/Archives Charmet/
The Bridgeman Art Library

MEDIUM: Lithograph

RELATED WORKS: Alphonse Mucha,
Cover of *La Plume*, 1897

unknown artist
Poster for *Bisleri Liqueur*, 1904
© Private Collection/The Bridgeman
Art Library

MEDIUM: Lithograph

RELATED WORKS: Alphonse Mucha,
Poster for *Bénédictine Liqueur*, 1896

symbols of natural plant forms to surround the centre portrait.
A street gas lamp was placed outside the theatrical set. This
work gave Mataloni recognition as an Art Nouveau practitioner.
A poster created nine years later in 1904, for *Bisleri Liqueur* (artist
unknown) (*see* right), utilizes aspects of Art Nouveau design. It
has flat picture space, a use of bold colour, abstract plant forms
to highlight the product name, and a young woman in flowing
dress, accompanied by a roaring lion.

Art Nouveau Origins in Italy

For an Italian contribution to Art Nouveau it is perhaps to the
Romanesque buildings of Italy that one should look. Here are
rich carvings, particularly in organic displays of plant and animal
life. This craftwork influenced artists, architects and art theorists.
Notably, one could consider the rhetoric of art critic and social
reformer John Ruskin (1819–1900) discussing the decorative
detail of *Palazzo Ducale* or the Cathedral of St Marks, in the
city of Venice. His love of Medieval Gothic, as the one true
architecture, supported the Gothic Revival and revealed Ruskin's
preference for organic designs, crafted in stone and wood, taken
from nature, and created by master masons in the medieval
period. Arthur Heygate Mackmurdo (1851–1942), who
accompanied Ruskin on a visit to Florence in 1874, created one
of the earliest prototype pieces of Art Nouveau with his woodcut
of *Wren's City Churches* in 1883 (*see* page 58). Mackmurdo stayed in
Italy for two years. His sketchbooks reveal studies of plant forms
taken from the capitals and decorative detail found in
Romanesque buildings. Soon after his return to London he
produced wallpaper, a chair design and book illustration,
noticeably influenced by Medieval Gothic plant forms.

Leonardo Bistolfi (1859–1933)
Manifesto for the Turin Exposition, 1902
© Civica Raccolta Stampe Bertarelli, Milan,
Italy/The Bridgeman Art Library

MEDIUM: unknown

RELATED WORKS: Raoul-François
Larche, *Loïe Fuller*, *c.* 1900

The Futurists

In the first decade of the twentieth century young Italian artists were calling for style, without historicism. It was a 'death knell' for Art Nouveau. 'Futurists' wanted new design, not old. Their ideas took shape in artists' communes and in the publication of manifestos. In Paris on 20 February 1909, the Italian Futurists, a group of poets, artists, designers and architects, took the front page of the French newspaper *Le Figaro* to announce their 'Futurist Manifesto' to the world. Although Italian by birth they recognized Paris as the centre of the arts and literary world. The group, led by poet Filippo Tommaso Marinetti (1876–1944), wanted to throw off the old century and historicism: 'we want no part of it, the past,' he said. Instead they wanted to concentrate on the new world of technology where speed dominated. The Italian Futurists (1909–18) worked towards new art forms and structures using new materials, to combine with socialist theory and the aggrandisement of war. The irony was that Europe went to war in 1914 with huge losses of life, including the lives of some members of the group.

Antoni Gaudí

In Spain, one man stands out. His name is Antoni Gaudí (1852–1926). He was born in the province of Tarragona in southern Catalonia, Spain. It is Gaudí's architecture that 'shouts' Art Nouveau, and yet what is it that identifies it with the works of other architects such as Charles Rennie Mackintosh (1868–1928), or Horta, Guimard or van de Velde? He, like them, used a free-form plan to create the building exterior. He used

Antoni Gaudí
Padouk armchair, c. 1902
© Private Collection/Photo © Christie's
Images/The Bridgeman Art Library

MEDIUM: Wood

RELATED WORKS: Antoni Gaudí, *Wooden bench*, designed for *Santa Coloma de Cervelló*, *Church of Colònia Güell*, 1898–1914

Antoni Gaudí
Exterior of the Casa Battló apartments, 1905–07
© Foundry Arts/Photographer: Hugh Palmer

MEDIUM: Architecture

RELATED WORKS: Antoni Gaudí, *Wooden bench for Casa Cavalet*, 1898–99

a mix of styles to create innovative houses and apartments in modern materials. Concrete, cast and wrought iron are used to shape the buildings and to decorate them. The feature that stands Gaudí's architecture apart from many of his counterparts is his lavish use of decorative art. His building designs, such as the *Casa Battló apartments*, 1905–07 (*see* right), in Barcelona, are mystical works. Gaudí remodelled the earlier 1875 building, creating a façade, roof and interior space. The exterior of the building is on two levels; it has symmetrical windows on each floor but Gaudí adds skull masks as balconies to some, but not all, window frames. The 'skulls' are spread asymmetrically, to break up the uniformity of the building outline. Other windows and openings are decorated with lengths of 'bone', to accentuate the supporting pillars. These are the colour of sea coral and mirror Gaudí's interest in marine life. The façade is covered with coloured mosaics to add a further visual dimension. The roof is adorned with sections of glazed fish scales and giant chimneys, in organic shapes, not quite marine life, not quite plant life. It is the very substance of Art Nouveau through its use of historicism, colour, curving forms and asymmetric plan.

Gaudí Interiors

The interior of the *Casa Battló* uses light, space and bright colour to 'decorate' the space. It is filled with curving forms and organic shapes. Gaudí designed the furniture, stained glass, fireplaces, floor tiles, doors and ironwork. This approach, to create a whole experience (exterior, interior and decorative furnishings), can be taken back to the aspiring Arts and Crafts movement in England. It can also be taken forward to early twentieth-century America,

where the American architect and decorative-arts designer, Frank Lloyd Wright (1867–1956) built his house *Taliesin*, in 1911, near Spring Green, Wisconsin, USA, designing every detail. Like Wright's furniture, which expressed the organic shape of the building, so too did Gaudí's designs for chairs and other pieces of furniture, for which he used exotic woods, such as padouk (*see Padouk armchair, c.* 1902, left).

The little Lilies of the Vale,
White ladies delicate & pale;

Origins of English Art Nouveau

Historians of art, design and architecture can trace the roots of Art Nouveau back to the mid-1850s in England. The Great Exhibition of the Works of Industry of all Nations dubbed 'The Great Exhibition' of 1851, held in Hyde Park, London, was a six-month showcase of the world's latest engineering, arts and crafts design. Exhibitors included the designer and architect Augustus Welby Northmore Pugin (1812–52) with his display of stained glass and ironware. A young man William Morris (1834–96) shunned the modernity of industrial design shown at the exhibition – he was one of the few Londoners who did not attend – and together with a group of colleagues formed William Morris and Co. to create handmade furniture, stained glass and craft works, which were on sale at the 1862 International Exhibition in London. At the same exhibition Japanese goods were on display.

A 'Battle of Styles'

In the early nineteenth century, architects of Britain had engrossed themselves in 'the battle of the styles' between Classical and Gothic-style architecture, led by the Catholic convert Pugin who desired a return to the Gothic style in place of pagan architecture. Stemming from this, the Arts and Crafts movement had its beginnings, led by Morris and his group of friends: the architect Philip Webb (1831–1915) and the Pre-Raphaelite painters including Dante Gabriel Rossetti (1828–82) and Edward Burne-Jones (1833–98), who identified with an era before industrialization, the England of medieval times. Their paintings, furniture and interior decoration embraced this love of the past, when the whole fabric of society relied on the 'handmade'. Before industrialization artisans and master craftsmen, using skills handed down through generations,

Walter Crane
Lilies of the Vale, **from** *Flora's Feast*,
c. 1889–1901
© Private Collection/The Stapleton
Collection/The Bridgeman Art Library

MEDIUM: Lithograph

RELATED WORKS: Walter Crane,
Illustrations for *Grimm's Fairy Tales*, 1882

made the most-creative furniture and clothing, tapestries and rugs, ceramics and metalwork. Meanwhile Christopher Dresser (1834–1904), in conjunction with a superb craftsman Archibald Knox (1864–1933), produced astonishing silverware and craft pieces, influenced by Knox's interest in his Celtic roots (he was born on the Isle of Man) and Dresser's love of Japanese design. Decorative pieces designed by Morris, Knox and Dresser were on sale at the new department store Liberty, which opened in London's Regent Street in 1875. The commercial expertise and entrepreneurial skills of the owner, Arthur Lazenby Liberty (1843–1935), brought together the Arts and Crafts aesthetic with the craze for oriental design. He opened a second store in Paris in 1890. The decorative wares on sale had their design roots in the Orient, Celtic Britain and the Arts and Crafts movement. It was known as *Stile Liberty*. His commercial promotion of decorative design, on desirable items for the fashionable and wealthy, can be seen as one of the prominent and pivotal strands of Art Nouveau that flourished at its peak from 1890 to 1905.

Guild, Commune and Studio

From the foundation of Morris's own design group and his socialist ideal of a better life through craftsmanship, many arts guilds and arts communes were formed in Britain and across Northern Europe. In England they included the Arts Workers Guild, formed by friend and associate of Morris, Walter Crane, in 1884. Crane was a talented book illustrator and ceramicist and a designer of many decorative artworks from stained glass to wallpaper. The guilds sprang up to combine and pool the talents of artists and craftsmen. These early communes and guilds were the forerunners of the Bauhaus School in Germany formed in Weimar in 1919, with its first director Walter Gropius (1883–1969). The Arts and Crafts Exhibition Society, which Crane developed with Lewis F. Day (1845–1910) in 1888, promoted artisans works, including Charles Robert Ashbee (1863–1942) and his Guild and School of Handicraft, at Toynbee Hall, a key inspiration for the *Wiener Werkstätte*. The commune lifestyle was one method for new movements and new artworks to gain notice. Crane would later decry the Art Nouveau movement, when it had become, in his eyes, commercial, cheap and badly designed, but his illustrations for *Flora's Feast*, *c.* 1889–1901 (*see* left), are clearly an illumination for artists inspired by Art Nouveau. Crane combines wind-blown hair, flowing Roman robes and long garlands of flowers to portray a young woman dancing to the floral rhythms of the seasons. These works are reminiscent of the graphic poster art produced by Mucha and others in Paris a few years later.

Arthur Heygate Mackmurdo

Another pioneer of Art Nouveau was Mackmurdo who worked as an architect, artist and designer. He was a true craftsman in the traditional style. One can see in his designs the influence of another great illustrator, William Blake (1757–1857), whose designs for *Songs of Innocence*, 1789, influenced Mackmurdo and certainly point towards an even earlier origin for Art Nouveau. The 1883 title page of *Wren's City Churches* (*see* right), a woodcut on handmade paper, by Mackmurdo used a series of whiplash lines to portray curling flames of fire. The asymmetrical flames move upward engulfing the page, perhaps to symbolize how the 1666 Fire of London had initiated the rebuilding of many parish churches by Sir Christopher Wren (1632–1723). Many art historians consider this to be the very first Art Nouveau artwork. Mackmurdo's designs for furniture and wallpaper followed the same form. Like the flames of the fire, Mackmurdo created a unique design based on unfurling shoots of plants, which curl and sway upward towards the light,

to create an astonishing piece of decorative fretwork in mahogany wood – a splay back inset for a *Mahogany chair, c.* 1883 (*see* left). This design, the first of its kind, is prototype and pivotal to Art Nouveau. Mackmurdo reproduced a similar design for *Thorns and Butterflies wallpaper, c.* 1886.

Arthur H. Mackmurdo
Mahogany chair, c. 1883
© Estate of A.H. Mackmurdo/
TopFoto/Woodmansterne

MEDIUM: Mahogany, with inset mahogany fretwork panel

RELATED WORKS: William Blake (1757–1827), Illustration for *The Book of Job: Job's Evil Dreams*, 1825 (reprinted 1874)

Arthur H. Mackmurdo
Title page of *Wren's City Churches*, 1883
© Estate of A.H. Mackmurdo/Victoria & Albert Museum, London, UK/ The Bridgeman Art Library

MEDIUM: unknown

RELATED WORKS: William Blake (1757–1827), Title page of *Songs of Innocence*, 1789

The Yellow Book

The fusion of Japanese design and Arts and Crafts aesthetic created a fashion for Japanese clothing and wallpapers, furniture and craft ware. The desire to decorate the drawing rooms of England in variations of it produced a compact band of followers, known as the Aesthetes. At the same time, wordy and worthy pamphlets, journals and books, many promoting the socialist message, were produced on hand-cranked presses, to the amusement of some who saw the whole movement as strictly for the richest members of society. A young man, Aubrey Beardsley (1872–98) capitalized on it. He created a series of drawings for a new arts journal, *The Yellow Book*, from 1894 to 1897. Some were reproduced as publicity posters (*see* below). Beardsley sold illustrations to *The Studio* magazine, too. One work clarifies this bonding of interest in Orientalism with the art communes of England, namely Beardsley's advertising poster for *A Comedy of Sighs*, 1894 (*see* right), a play by John Todhunter (1839–1916). In the poster a young woman, portrayed full length, wears the loose-fitting clothing style of the Pre-Raphaelite maiden; her hair is worn long and it flows back over her shoulders. The flat porcelain doll image is in blue and white – the favoured porcelain of the Aesthetes – overlaid with small yellow spots. At top right, the theatre location, the 'Avenue Theatre' has its name in a distinctly oriental typeface. Beardsley's career was short lived – he died at the age of 26 – but his work, like a young Masaccio

(*c.* 1400–28) in Renaissance Florence, influenced a generation of artists and consolidated interest in this new art form. His fusion of flat, two-dimensional illustration was sparingly cut back to outline drawing and it is beautifully illustrated in Beardsley's *Isolde*, an 1895 illustration for *The Studio* (*see* pages 60–61).

Aubrey Beardsley
Poster for *A Comedy of Sighs*, 1894
© Victoria & Albert Museum, London,
UK/The Bridgeman Art Library

MEDIUM: unknown

RELATED WORKS: Walter Crane,
Illustrations for *Flora's Feast*, *c.* 1889–1901

Aubrey Beardsley
Poster for *The Yellow Book*, 1894–97
© Victoria & Albert Museum, London,
UK/The Bridgeman Art Library

MEDIUM: unknown

RELATED WORKS: J.M. Whistler
(1834–1903), *La Princesse du Pays de la
Porcelaine*, 1863–64

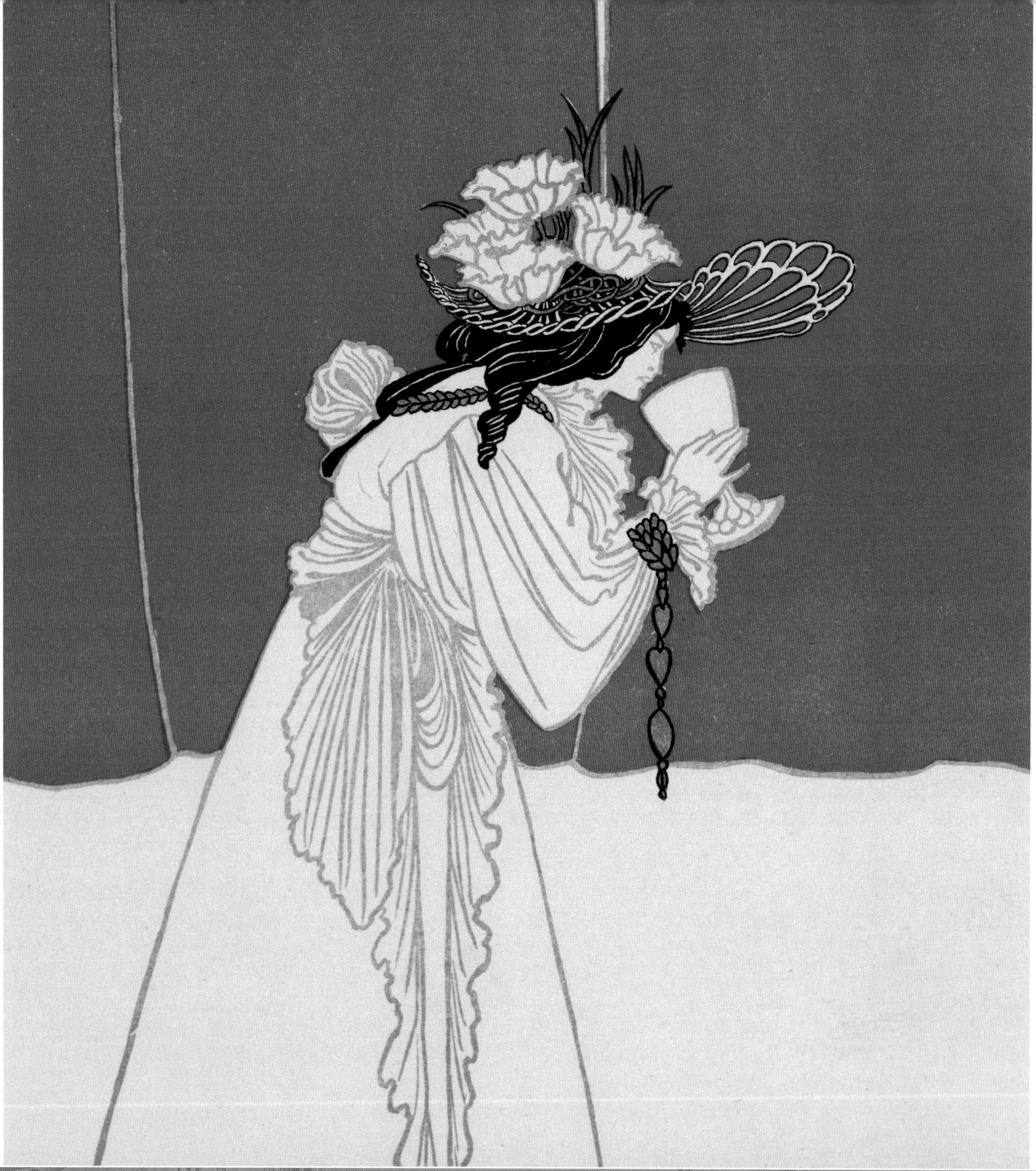

Peacocks and Sunflowers

ISOLDE

Beardsley's style in some respect followed on from the plumes of flame and the organic plant-tendril forms of Mackmurdo, yet the people portrayed by Beardsley were often the style-driven Aesthetes, caught up in a wave of nostalgia and commerce. In constant use by decorative designers, the eye of fashionable peacock plumes, along with a yellow-sunflower motif, adorned the homes of the wealthy Aesthetes. Peacock feathers, sunflowers and variegated plant forms were favoured forms of decorative design for handmade wallpapers, expensive rugs and soft furnishings, and were used in graphic art. A typical example is the wind-tossed tendrils, stems and flower heads that stretch upward in Beardsley's sketch to illustrate the cover of *Salomé, c.* 1894 (*see* right), by the author, poet, playwright and Aesthete Oscar Wilde (1854–1900).

Scottish Architecture and Design

In Scotland the organic plant forms and geometric purity of Japanese design found favour with the architect Charles Rennie Mackintosh. His architectural style is unique. It borrows from Scotland's baronial past with the turrets and towers of its distinctive castles, yet is neither historic nor truly modern. Mackintosh combined powerful geometric forms to create a new architectural style. For decorative design, he worked alongside his wife Margaret MacDonald (1864–1933), her sister Frances

Aubrey Beardsley
Isolde, illustration for *The Studio,* 1895
© Private Collection/The Stapleton
Collection/The Bridgeman Art Library

MEDIUM: Lithograph

RELATED WORKS: Eugène Grasset,
Avril, calendar page, 1896

Aubrey Beardsley
Cover of *Salomé, c.* 1894
© Private Collection/The Stapleton
Collection/The Bridgeman Art Library

MEDIUM: Ink on paper

RELATED WORKS: Aubrey Beardsley,
Cover of *The Yellow Book*, October 1894

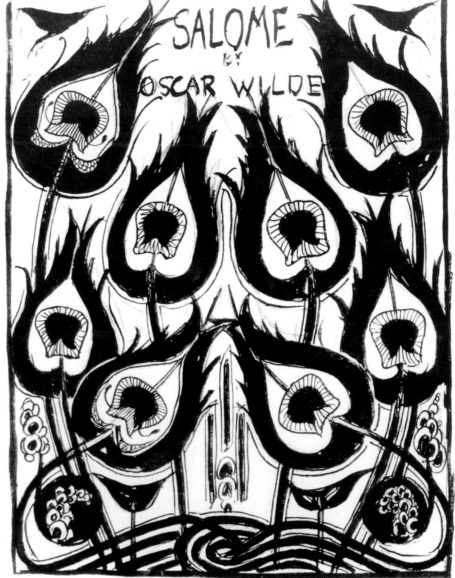

62

(1873–1921) and Frances's husband James Herbert MacNair (1868–1955), all friends, to achieve a unity of design and decorative furnishings in wood and metal. They were called the 'Glasgow Four'. Mackintosh's illustrations in watercolour would be often transferred to decorate furniture. *The Wassail*, 1900 (*see* right), a work in watercolour and pencil on paper, utilizes the flat space of Japanese line. Its content is a combination of Beardsley's stylized women and Celtic iconography.

A Partnership of Talent

Looking at the remarkable items of furniture designed by Mackintosh for commissioned interiors, the refurbishment of four tea rooms in Glasgow owned by Kate Cranston (1850–1934) gave Mackintosh scope for interior and exterior design from 1897 to 1917. *The Willow Tea Rooms* at 217 Sauchiehall Street were the first to be completely designed by Mackintosh: interior, exterior and furnishings in 1903. *The Hill House*, 1902–04, overlooking the River Clyde is now considered Mackintosh's finest interior design. Of particular note, on many items of furniture, are the painted insets by the MacDonald sisters. A *Painted oak cabinet*, custom-made for 14 Kingsborough Gardens, Glasgow in 1902 (*see* left), shows how Mackintosh created furniture as an integral part of the interior design and architectural form. The cabinet is decoratively colourful yet sparse with strong, clean lines. Two young women are depicted on the inner sides of the doors. They hold jewel-like globes in elongated matchstick arms. They are clothed in pseudo-oriental robes, shaped like a retracted bird wing. The pared-back single-plane form creates design pattern rather than human shape. Mackintosh's room interiors and decorative furniture appeared in arts journals of the period, which were

Charles Rennie Mackintosh
Painted oak cabinet, for 14 Kingsborough Gardens, Glasgow, 1902
© The Fine Art Society, London, UK/ The Bridgeman Art Library

MEDIUM: Painted oak

RELATED WORKS: Gustav Klimt, *Die Hoffnung II (Hope II)*, 1907–08

Charles Rennie Mackintosh
The Wassail (detail), 1900
© Private Collection/Photo © Christie's Images/The Bridgeman Art Library

MEDIUM: Watercolour and pencil on paper

RELATED WORKS: Aubrey Beardsley, *Messalina*, c. 1897

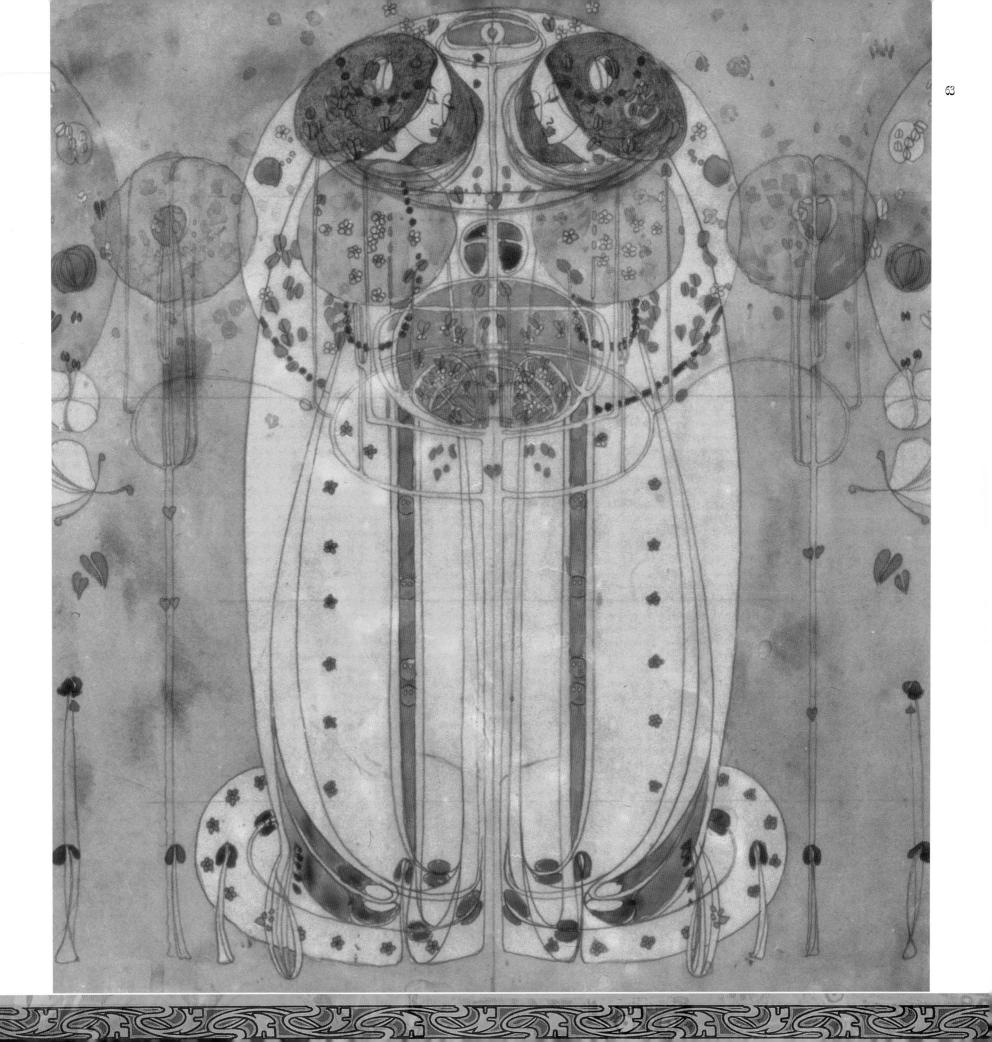

distributed across Europe. This led to an exhibition of his work in Belgium and furthered interest in his architectural style and design form. He was one of the designers whom Hermann Muthesius (1861–1927), an attaché to the German Embassy in London from 1896 to 1903, picked out as examples of good British design, for Muthesius' 1904 publication *Das Englische Haus*. Mackintosh's paintings, designs for jewellery, furnishings and furniture are recognized as specific contributors to the Art Nouveau movement.

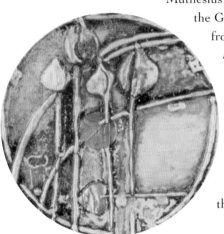

It has to be Tiffany

One name above all others defines the Art Nouveau movement in the United States of America, and it is found in the medium of glassware, particularly leaded-glass lampshades, designed by Tiffany Studios, the brainchild of Louis Comfort Tiffany (1848–1933). The company made many designs in glass, including popular stained-glass insets, such as the *Parakeets and Goldfish Bowl*, *c.* 1893 (*see* right), a leaded and plate-glass window. Tiffany attracted the same kind of customers who had flocked to Morris's Oxford Street store on the other side of the Atlantic: the Aesthetes and the passionate collectors of Art Nouveau.

Tiffany Studios created a plethora of stained-glass windows and lamps, blown glass and mosaics, enamels, metalwork, jewellery and ceramics to satisfy demand for their Art Nouveau creations.

Margaret MacDonald Mackintosh
The Opera of the Wind, c. 1902
© Private Collection/© The Fine Art Society, London, UK/The Bridgeman Art Library

MEDIUM: Inlaid gesso panel

RELATED WORKS: Margaret MacDonald Mackintosh, *The Opera of the Sea, c.* 1902

Louis Comfort Tiffany
Parakeets and Goldfish Bowl (detail), *c.* 1893
© Private Collection/Photo © Christie's Images/The Bridgeman Art Library

MEDIUM: Stained glass

RELATED WORKS: Louis Comfort Tiffany, *Magnolias and Irises* (leaded Favrile glass), *c.* 1908

William H. Bradley
Poster for *The Chap Book,*
date unknown
© Estate of William H. Bradley/Private
Collection/The Bridgeman Art Library

MEDIUM: unknown

RELATED WORKS: Frank Hazenplug
(b. 1873), Cover of *The Chap Book*, 1899

William H. Bradley
Poster for *The Inland Printer,*
Christmas 1895 issue
© Estate of William H. Bradley/Private
Collection/The Stapleton Collection/
The Bridgeman Art Library

MEDIUM: Lithograph

RELATED WORKS: Maurice Prendergast
(b. 1858), *The Red Cape*, 1891–94

William H. Bradley

At the age of 12, Will(iam) H. Bradley (1868–1962) gained
experience as a printer at a newspaper office in his home town
of Boston, Massachusetts. He took his experiences on to Chicago
where he held various jobs as a typesetter and wood engraver.
In 1893 he opened his own studio and concentrated on design,
working for companies such as *Vogue* magazine and *Ladies Home
Journal*. He had seen the drawings of Beardsley and of Grasset,
which encouraged him to continue developing his own style.
His use of bold sinuous lines created an epithet for him as the
'American Beardsley', which is grossly inaccurate since Bradley
had established his own style beforehand. By the mid-1890s he
was publishing his own magazine *Bradley: His Book*, a compilation
of anecdotes, poetry and illustration as well as typography and
printing. Between 1894 and 1898, Bradley was also involved in
the publication *The Chap Book* along the same lines. It was the
bold and colourful posters he created to promote the journal (*see
left*) that established his reputation as the artist who brought Art
Nouveau to America. The posters, used to promote the journal
on newsstands, were avidly collected at the time.

The Inland Printer

Bradley also designed covers and posters for other journals
such as the trade magazine *The Inland Printer*, which ensured
his reputation in France after Bing saw it. The clever but simple
design for the *Christmas 1895 issue* (*see right*) exemplifies Bradley's
adherence to the prevalent Art Nouveau style but with his own
twist. *The Inland Printer* was an extremely important journal for

disseminating graphic arts in the USA. It began in 1883 as a 24-page magazine but by 1900 it had increased to over 200 pages, such were the importance of new technologies and the role of the new opportunities for printing, particularly in the consumer market. The journal continues to be published in Chicago as *The American Printer and Lithographer*. The lettering used in the poster was adopted by a number of typographers in America and Germany. The American Type Founders Company paid a commission to Bradley, naming the typeface after him. In 1915, Bradley became artistic director for the Hearst Corporation. In the 1950s he created his own memoir *Bradley: His Chap Book* and continued working up to his death aged 94.

Louis John Rhead

In contrast, a poster by the American graphic artist Louis John Rhead (1857–1926), advertising *The Sun*, an American newspaper (*see* left and right), portrays a young woman in right profile, standing in parkland with the sun rising to her left. An arabesque curve crosses the picture plane defining the road towards the sun. The woman wears a rich, full-length cloak. Her flame-coloured hair tumbles over her shoulders. Two rows of flowerheads are at her feet. Rhead's use of Japanese line and bold colour, plus the varied typography, are traits of Art Nouveau, beautifully expressed in this poster work, which uses the flat space of the Japanese print.

Louis John Rhead
Poster for *The Sun*, date unknown
© Private Collection/The Stapleton
Collection/The Bridgeman Art Library

MEDIUM: Lithograph

RELATED WORKS: Alphonse Mucha,
Poster for *La Dame aux Camélias*, 1896

Decline and Renewal

By 1910 the main protagonists of the loosely formed, widely dispersed group of artists, designers and architects, collectively producing works of Art Nouveau had established their names with the decorative movement but were finding fewer patrons to commission their work. The fashion and passion for Art Nouveau were running out of steam in Europe and some artists, such as Mucha, moved to America to capitalize on the growth of interest in Art Nouveau in the USA.

Last Throes of Art Nouveau

In Paris, a young Frenchman, Marcel Duchamp (1887–1968), created his *Bicycle Wheel*, in 1913. It was a 'ready-made' piece of artwork from a found object. It was to scandalize the arts world and shift focus away from stylized decorative art. The once avant-garde Art Nouveau movement lost momentum during this period. Whilst the purity of Japanese geometric line and form continued, interest in decorative wares, posters and advertisements with flat-surface style and sinuous wavy lines faltered. Cheap copies of Tiffany-style lamps and other ephemera associated with its form led the wealthy middle classes to look for new fashion and new interiors. Whilst Art Nouveau continued in America, it emerged post-First World War in Europe in 1918 as *Arts Décoratifs*, now called Art Deco. This refined, more feminine, form of decorative design created a new wave of designers happy to create new fashions, furniture, furnishings, jewellery and architectural decoration to lure patrons. It zenith was perhaps at the Paris Exposition of 1925 (the *Exposition Internationale des Arts Décoratifs et Industriels Modernes*). Here the last vestiges of Art Nouveau mixed with the more desirable, highly fashionable Art Deco. Meanwhile in a far corner of the exposition, loathed by the organizers but admired by the emerging artists, designers and architects, the new avant-garde appeared. It was the *Pavilion de L'Esprit Nouveau*: a very plain stark-white cube-shape house, designed by Charles-Édouard Jeanneret (1887–1965), a Swiss painter, furniture designer and architect, better known as Le Corbusier. Its appearance was to herald the subsequent decline of interest in Art Deco and with it the last strands of Art Nouveau.

Art Nouveau

Section Two

The Graphic Arts

Showcasing the main practitioners of fin-de-siècle graphic arts and their iconic creations of the time.

JULES CHÉRET
(1836–1932)

The 'Master' of Poster Design

Jules Chéret (1836–1932) was born in Paris to a family of artisans. Lack of funding meant that Chéret's formal education ended at 13 years of age, but the knowledge he gained within family circles, regarding art and design, would lead him towards a successful career in graphic art. On leaving school Chéret began a three-year apprenticeship with a lithographer who was known to his father, and he took a course in drawing at the École Nationale de Dessin in Paris, under Horace Lecoq de Boisbaudran (1802–97). Beginning work as a professional graphic artist he sold only a few designs initially, to illustrators and music publishers. He decided to travel to London to expand his opportunities and there he worked for the Maple Furniture Company, creating drawings for furniture design. It did not inspire him, however, and he returned to Paris, to pursue his career and it was here that the first strands of his future success were hinted at when he created the poster *Orpheus in the Underworld*, 1858, for the music composer Jacques Offenbach (1819–80). This did not immediately lead to more work, and so Chéret headed for London once more and from 1859 to 1866 he spent his time in the city designing book jackets and publicity posters.

Raoul-François Larche
Loïe Fuller, c. 1900
Private Collection/Photo © Christie's
Images/The Bridgeman Art Library

MEDIUM: Bronze

RELATED WORKS:
Peter Behrens, *Table lamp,* 1902

Jules Chéret
Poster for *Folies-Bergère:*
La Loïe Fuller, 1893
© Private Collection/The Stapleton
Collection/The Bridgeman Art Library

MEDIUM: Lithograph

RELATED WORKS: Georges de Feure,
Poster for *Loïe Fuller,* 1904

FOLIES·BERGÈRE

La Loïe Fuller

Jules Chéret
Poster for *Vin Mariani*, 1894
© Private Collection/Archives Charmet/
The Bridgeman Art Library

MEDIUM: Lithograph

RELATED WORKS: Dudley Hardy
(1865–1922), Poster for *'A Gaiety Girl'*, 1893

Jules Chéret
Poster for *Palais de Glace*, 1896
© Private Collection/The Stapleton
Collection/The Bridgeman Art Library

MEDIUM: Lithograph

RELATED WORKS: Robert Wildhack
(1881–1940), Cover for *Scribner's*,
March, 1907

Chéret and Rimmel

In this early part of Chéret's career one can see, in his expectations
and frustrations, a talented graphic artist who needed to find a
suitable client to allow him to create something unique. Chéret had
the talent, he needed the right opportunity. In London, through a
friend, he had met Eugene Rimmel (1820–87), the successful French
perfume and toiletries manufacturer. Rimmel employed him to
design some of the company's publicity. The major breakthrough
came, however, when Rimmel backed Chéret in an enterprise to set
up a colour lithography shop in Paris in 1866, the first of its kind.
The machine itself had to be imported from London. Owning his
own print establishment, Chéret seized the opportunity to design
and print posters as he wanted them to be. At first he worked in
two colours and in 1869 introduced three: using black, red and a
combination colour. He worked directly on to the stones, in a variety
of methods, including stipple, crosshatching and a 'wash' that
produced soft, flat colour. It was at this time that many theories on
colour were being discussed in academic papers and publications,
focusing on complementary colour forms. Chéret was at the heart
of it and his own poster designs delighted advertisers. This 'gamble'
by Rimmel paid off and brought Chéret to the attention of the whole
of Paris. It sealed his career and his unique 'Chéret' poster style.

Joie de Vivre!

Chéret's posters for music halls and theatres were often based on
the frivolous scenes painted by the eighteenth-century French artist
Antoine Watteau (1684–1721). His Rococo *joie de vivre* style became
very popular and he was soon being commissioned to create
advertising posters for other products, such as toiletries, household

goods and wines. The women depicted in Chéret's posters are idealized, unlike the *demi-mondaines* depicted in contemporary paintings by Edgar Degas (1834–1917) and Édouard Manet (1832–83). There is a naivety in Chéret's figures, which became known as his 'Chérettes', a somewhat liberating model for many ordinary Parisian women. The development of the curvilinear forms associated with the Art Nouveau style emanate in part from the dynamic forms of dance at the turn of the nineteenth into the twentieth century. Dancers that included Isadora Duncan (1877–1927) and Loïe Fuller (1862–1928) developed a more modern dance practice that eschewed conventional and classical forms. The dances were often exotic and even erotic

and the curvilinear forms were accentuated by their elaborate gowns. Chéret was one of several artists who created publicity posters to promote the dancers at famous nightclubs such as the Folies-Bergère. This nightspot already had a reputation in the 1880s for its entertainment, but dancers such as Fuller had taken it to a new level of outlandishness. Chéret captured her spirit in his 1893 poster *Folies-Bergère: La Loïe Fuller* (*see* page 73). She was not only publicized in print; Raoul-François Larche (1860–1912) caught her sensuous style too, in his gilded bronze sculpture of *Loïe Fuller*, c. 1900 (*see* page 72). Chéret used the same 'spirit' of popular dance in *Vin Mariani*, 1894 (*see* page 74), depicting a sprightly 'Chérette' in his poster for a French tonic.

A Sketcher of Modern Life

In 1896 Chéret was commissioned to produce a poster promoting the *Palais de Glace*. This was an ice-skating establishment and, unlike many other leisure enterprises, it was not considered inappropriate for young women to ice-skate unaccompanied. Chéret pushes that point in his poster *Palais de Glace*, 1896 (*see* page 75), which captures the free spirit of a young woman dancing on ice. He had the capacity to add 'life' to any image he depicted, even for home-cleaning products, and consequently his talent was much in demand from advertisers. Products were given the 'Chéret' touch to entice buyers. His masterful technique is typified, for example, in *Saxoléine*, 1896 (*see* left), an advertisement for paraffin oil, where his trademark 'Chérette' stands beautifully dressed, bathing in the bright glow of the lamp. Chéret's influence in poster design resonated around Paris in the 1890s. He was nicknamed the 'Master of Poster Design' and was the doyen of the discipline to emerging artists in Paris in the last quarter of the nineteenth century.

Jules Chéret
Poster for *Saxoléine*, 1896
© Private Collection/The Stapleton
Collection/The Bridgeman Art Library

MEDIUM: Lithograph

RELATED WORKS: Louis Anquetin
(1861–1932), Poster for *Le Rire*, 1894

Jules Chéret
Poster for *La Diaphane,*
translucent face powder, 1890
© Private Collection/The Stapleton
Collection/The Bridgeman Art Library

MEDIUM: Lithograph

RELATED WORKS: Emmanuel Orazi,
Portrait of Sarah Bernhardt, date unknown

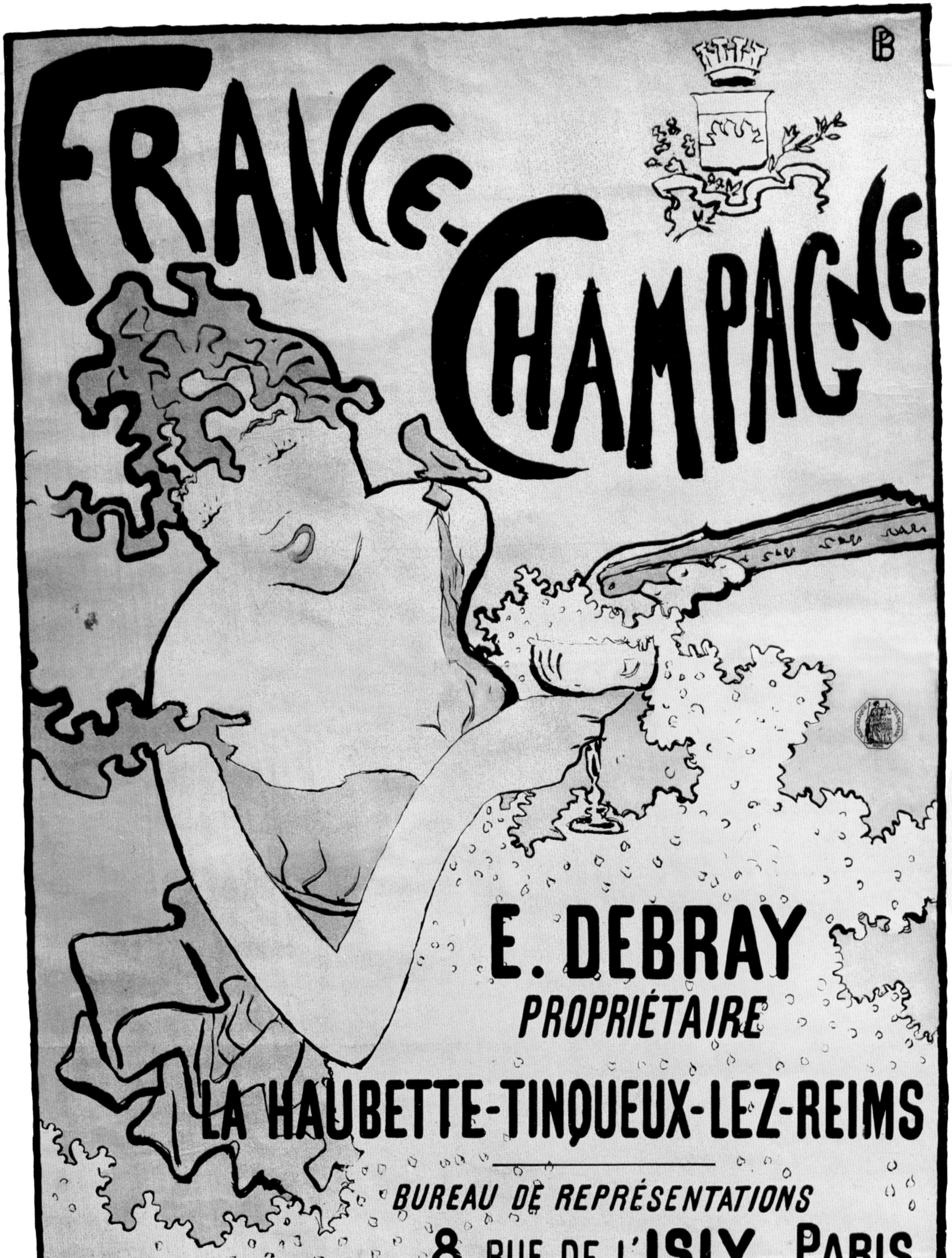

FRANCE-CHAMPAGNE
E. DEBRAY
PROPRIÉTAIRE
LA HAUBETTE-TINQUEUX-LEZ-REIMS
BUREAU DE REPRÉSENTATIONS
8, RUE DE L'ISLY PARIS

PIERRE BONNARD
(1867–1947)

Nouveau Graphic Style

Pierre Bonnard (1867–1947) was born in Fontenay-aux-Roses, a small commune in the southwestern suburbs of Paris, about six miles from the centre. His father, a civil servant, worked for the war ministry and was a respected public figure who expected his son, the second of three children, to study law. After graduating from high school in 1885, Bonnard studied law in Paris but his main interest was art, so in his spare time he attended the Académie Julian and the École des Beaux-Arts, making friends with other young artists such as Maurice Denis (1870–1943), Paul Sérusier (1865–1927), Édouard Vuillard (1868–1940) and Paul-Elie Ranson (1862–1909); and together they would form *Les Nabis*. Bonnard decided to make art his full-time profession in 1889 after he sold his first design, which he had created for a graphic-arts poster. Bonnard repeated this success with further lithographs for book illustrations, poster advertisements and artworks for publications such as *La Revue Blanche*. His design style became synonymous with Art Nouveau in Paris, typified by a poster he created for Reims champagne, *France-Champagne*, in 1891 (*see* left). It inspired Henri de Toulouse-Lautrec (1864–1901), amongst others, to exploit this art form, although Bonnard himself was later to move away from graphic art towards painting.

Pierre Bonnard
Poster for *France-Champagne*, 1891
Courtesy of Bibliotheque Nationale, Paris, France/Giraudon/The Bridgeman Art Library/© ADAGP, Paris and DACS, London 2009

MEDIUM: Lithograph

RELATED WORKS: Alphonse Mucha, Poster for *Job*, 1898

HENRI DE TOULOUSE-LAUTREC
(1864–1901)

Parisian Life

Toulouse-Lautrec was born to a wealthy aristocratic family, but suffered from a debilitating genetic disorder that left him crippled. In the 1880s he moved with his family to Paris and enrolled at an art academy alongside artists such as Emile Bernard (1868–1941), but it was his association with the Nabis painters, Bonnard and Vuillard, that set him on the path to illustration. With them he began to illustrate for *La Revue Blanche*, a popular magazine of the time. Despite his wealth, Toulouse-Lautrec set up a studio in Montmartre, a poor, squalid and dangerous part of the city in which many artists had established their studios because of the low rents. He was drawn to the everyday life of its inhabitants, which became inspiring subject matter for him, in particular its café society, seedy brothels and outlandish nightlife, where many of society's deviants gathered. He developed an iconoclastic view of bourgeois sensibilities and sentimentality, preferring instead to depict the debauchery of Parisian life, its protagonists such as the dancers and prostitutes becoming his friends. His lifestyle reflected the company he kept and he quickly became an alcoholic, dying at the relatively young age of 36.

The Moulin Rouge

Although influenced by Chéret and Bonnard, Toulouse-Lautrec's portrayals are less anonymous, even to the point of caricature. In his various portrayals set in the Moulin Rouge dance hall in Paris, he depicted, for example, Louise Weber (1866–1929) and

Henri de Toulouse-Lautrec
Poster for *La Goulue at the Moulin Rouge*, 1891
© Private Collection/The Stapleton Collection/The Bridgeman Art Library

MEDIUM: Lithograph

RELATED WORKS: Pierre Bonnard, *La Revue Blanche*, 1894

Henri de Toulouse-Lautrec
Poster for *Aristide Bruant at the Ambassadeurs*, 1892
© Bibliotheque Nationale, Paris, France/ The Bridgeman Art Library

MEDIUM: Lithograph

RELATED WORKS: Leonetto Cappiello (1875–1942), Poster for *'Polaire'*, 1910

her dance partner Jacques Renaudin (1843–1907), as a reflection of their respective nicknames, La Goulue (the glutton) and Valentin le Désossé (Valentine the boneless), (*see* left). The Moulin Rouge was opened in 1889 and very quickly gained a reputation as an exciting nightclub, particularly with acts such as La Goulue, who had earned her epithet through her voracious appetite, Jane Avril (1868–1943) and Yvette Guilbert (1867–1944), each of whom were immortalized in Toulouse-Lautrec's drawings and paintings. He had a loathing of bourgeois insincerity and hypocrisy and enjoyed the company of working-class people infinitely more. Because of his own appearance as a crippled dwarf, often shabbily dressed and drunk, he seemed to be more akin to the company he kept and, like the showgirls he associated with, he refused to hide from ridiculing staring eyes and instead became raucous in public himself.

The Café Concert Poster

Like Toulouse-Lautrec, Aristide Bruant (1851–1925) had come from a well-to-do family and had gravitated to Montmartre. Bruant became well known as a cabaret performer in Paris and appeared regularly at Le Chat Noir, a wild nightclub that had opened in 1881. His star turn, however, was at the *Ambassadeurs* and *Eldorado* café-concerts. For these, Bruant commissioned Toulouse-Lautrec to create the posters (*see* right), the two men becoming firm friends thereafter. By the time he was executing the posters for Bruant, Toulouse-Lautrec had achieved considerable success, particularly in his poster designs, and although he had a private income from his family, which itself

JANE
Avril

H.Stern, Paris.

1899

was adequate, he took a pride in making money from his art and even kept a separate account of his earnings. His main employer for posters was Boussod, Valadon & Cie, a firm of art dealers and print makers with whom he had his first one-man exhibition in 1895. The firm, linked also to Goupil's gallery, ensured the wider exposure of his work when it arranged an exhibition of Toulouse-Lautrec's graphic and fine-art works in London in 1898.

Jane Avril

Possibly the most well known and oft painted of all Toulouse-Lautrec's figures is that of the dancer Avril. She appeared as an audience member in his *Le Divan Japonais* poster of 1892 (*see* right), but also as a can-can dancer at the Moulin Rouge, 1899 (*see* left), her narrow-waist dresses marking a contrast to her predecessor La Goulue and which are more akin to the sinuous lines of Art Nouveau. The dancer commissioned many of the posters herself, such was her status in Paris at the time, and these posters were often reproduced as limited-edition lithographs printed on high-quality vellum or Japanese papers and sold as expensive collectors' items. This practice was in line with other artists and art dealers at the time seeking to exploit the saleability of such artwork. Avril and others around Toulouse-Lautrec were acutely aware of his alcoholism and he also suffered from syphilis, exacerbating his already erratic and eccentric behaviour, and from time to time Lautrec even lived in brothels. It was, however, his alcoholism that finally brought his short life to an end, but not before he had completed nearly 1,000 paintings and watercolours and over 300 designs for posters and fine-art prints.

Henri de Toulouse-Lautrec
Poster for *Jane Avril*, 1899
© Haags Gemeentemuseum, The Hague,
Netherlands/The Bridgeman Art Library

MEDIUM: Lithograph

RELATED WORKS: Maurice Biais
(1875–1926), Poster for *Jane Avril*, c. 1900

Henri de Toulouse-Lautrec
Poster for *Le Divan Japonais*, 1892
© Bibliotheque Nationale, Paris, France/
Lauros/Giraudon/The Bridgeman
Art Library

MEDIUM: Lithograph

RELATED WORKS: Georges de Feure,
Poster for *Salon des Cent*, 1894

Théophile-Alexandre Steinlen
Poster for *Lait pur stérilisé*
de la Vingeanne, 1894–95
© Bibliotheque des Arts Décoratifs,
Paris, France/Lauros/Giraudon/
The Bridgeman Art Library

MEDIUM: Lithograph

RELATED WORKS: John Everett
Millais (1829–96), *'Bubbles',* poster for
Pears soap, 1886

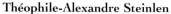

THÉOPHILE-ALEXANDRE STEINLEN
(1859–1923)

Everyday Subject Matter

In Paris during the 1890s, Théophile-Alexandre Steinlen
(1859–1923) was better known in his day than Toulouse-
Lautrec for illustration work. Swiss born, Steinlen came
to Montmartre in 1881 and rapidly became well known
as an artist moving in the same circles as Toulouse-Lautrec
and focusing on the everyday subject matter of the area.
He was, however, more politically active. He illustrated
the covers of *Chambard Socialiste* and *Feuille,* which were
empathetic to an anti-bourgeois socialist/anarchist cause.
His most-famous political poster was *Petit Sou,* executed
in 1900 and anticipating some of the revolutionary posters
of the 1920s. Steinlen also became the main illustrator for
Bruant's satirical magazine *Le Mirliton* and for his collections
of non-conformist songs. He created numerous advertising
posters using a heightened sense of realism to the images.
In his advertising poster for *Lait pur stérilisé de la Vingeanne,*
1894–95 (*see* left), Steinlen combined a number of Art Nouveau
elements in the work. The rectilinear chair, the billowing red
dress, the curvilinear typeface and the stylized cats with their
curled tails are all essential features of the style. Steinlen was
much revered when Pablo Picasso (1881–1973) first came
to Paris in 1900, and his early drawings leading up to the
so-called 'Blue Period' borrow heavily from Steinlen's.

Le Chat Noir

Probably the most-famous work for both the club and the artist is Steinlen's poster *Le Chat Noir Cabaret*, 1896 (*see* right), which is archetypal of the Art Nouveau style, particularly in its curved and asymmetrical text. Another work contemporary to this was *La Rue*, 1896 (*see* pages 86–87), a life-size poster of people of mixed classes in a Parisian street. The content is ambiguous, but does suggest the propositioning of women for sexual favours. The foil for this activity is in the young girl and is redolent of a similar scene in *Les Parapluies*, 1881–86 by Pierre-Auguste Renoir (1841–1919). At the turn of the century, Steinlen produced a number of erotic intimate etchings, sold in small limited editions; he also turned his hand to sculpture, producing a number of bronzes of cats. His final creative flowering was in a series of patriotic images during the First World War including *Gare de l'Est*, c. 1914–15, depicting a group of French soldiers saying goodbye to their loved ones before going to the Front.

Théophile-Alexandre Steinlen
Poster for *Le Chat Noir Cabaret*, 1896
© Private Collection/The Bridgeman Art Library

MEDIUM: Lithograph

RELATED WORKS: Édouard Manet (1832–83), *Olympia*, 1863

(overleaf)

Théophile-Alexandre Steinlen
La Rue, poster for *Charles Verneau*, 1896
© Private Collection/The Bridgeman Art Library

MEDIUM: Lithograph

RELATED WORKS: Théophile-Alexandre Steinlen, Poster for *Compagnie Francaise des Chocolats et des Thés*, c. 1896–98

ARLE SVERNEAU

AFFICHES CHARLE SVERNEAU

LA RUE   CHARLES VERNEAU, IMP.

ALPHONSE MUCHA
(1860-1939)

Slavic Origins

Alphonse Mucha (1860–1939) was born in the town of Ivančice in southern Moravia (now the Czech Republic) on 24 July 1860. He was the eldest of three children to his father's second wife. His father worked as a court official at the Imperial and District Court in the town and the Mucha family included three further children, from his father's first marriage. Mucha's early interests spanned

the church, music, choral singing and art. His mother wanted him to be a priest, which Mucha did consider for a short time, and his superb singing voice gave him a place at choir school, which allowed him a paid education until his early teens. However, it was art that would be the eventual winner; he was known to have been able to draw before he could walk. After leaving school at 15, for failing to complete his studies in time, his father found him a clerical job in the Imperial and District Court, but Mucha knew that he was meant to be an artist. At 19 he left the civil service and found work as a theatrical-scene painter. This type of work, creating stage sets, gave him experience of large-scale decorative work.

Alphonse Mucha
Poster for *Gismonda*, 1894
© Mucha Trust 2009

MEDIUM: Lithograph

RELATED WORKS:
William Nicholson (1872–1949),
Poster for *Sarah Bernhardt*, 1897

René Lalique
Pendant brooch designed as two dragonflies, c. 1895–1900
Courtesy of Christie's Images Ltd/
© ADAGP, Paris and DACS, London 2009

MEDIUM: Diamond, tourmaline and *plique-à-jour* enamel

RELATED WORKS: Philippe Wolfers,
Necklace, 1898

A Generous Sponsor

Luck always seemed to be part of Mucha's life. In 1881, one chance meeting led to an extensive commission from Count Karl Khuen-Belassi (1849–1918), the owner of Emmerhof Castle in Hrušovany. Mucha decorated several rooms of the count's baronial home with mural paintings and restored some of the family portraits. This led Mucha to work for another family member, Count Egon (1849–1909). At this count's home, a chance meeting with the notable artist Professor Wilhelm Kray (1828–89) of the Munich Academy of Arts led Egon to sponsor Mucha to train as an artist at the Munich Academy for two years. This was a defining moment in Mucha's life, one that allowed him to transform from a naturally gifted painter to a trained artist. In 1887 Mucha moved to Paris, sponsored by the count, and attended the Académie Julian, where he met fellow artists. However, luck ran out when the count's sponsorship abruptly stopped in 1889 and Mucha was forced

to take any work he could. For some time he lived as an impoverished artist in a garret room, eating a frugal diet of beans and soup, but eventually, as an accomplished and gifted draughtsman, he gained work as an illustrator and by 1891 existed on commercial-art work, including book illustrations and calendars. His circle of friends included Paul Gauguin (1848–1903) and members of the Nabis.

Alphonse Mucha
Zodiac, 1896
© Mucha Trust 2009

MEDIUM: Lithograph

RELATED WORKS: Anthony Sandys (1829–1904), *Love's Shadow*, 1867

Victor Horta
Bannister from the Hôtel Sôlvay, Brussels, 1894
© Estate of Victor Horta/The Bridgeman Art Library

MEDIUM: unknown

RELATED WORKS: Paul Hankar (1859–1901), *Shop front*, 1900

Alphonse Mucha
Poster for *Monaco-Monte-Carlo*, 1897
© Mucha Trust 2009

MEDIUM: Lithograph

RELATED WORKS: Eugène Grasset,
Poster for *L'Encre Marquet*, 1892

Gismonda

In late December 1894 Mucha, not having enough money to
return home to see his family, agreed to help an artist friend by
checking his illustration proofs at the print publishing house of
Lemercier. Everyone had left Paris to go home for the seasonal
holiday. A late call to Lemercier from the office of the French
theatrical star Sarah Bernhardt (1844–1923) proved Mucha's
luck once again. Unhappy with a publicity poster illustrating
her latest play production, *Gismonda*, she wanted a replacement.
Lemercier needed a graphic artist and Mucha stepped in to
design his first poster. He visited the theatre to watch Bernhardt
in the play and then created a poster for it (*see* pages 88–89).
His creativity in designing the poster, not only in the depiction
of Bernhardt in the title role, but the radical, full-length format,
meant that the poster would be the most significant commission
of his career. Bernhardt was ecstatic when she saw it and
immediately signed him to a five-year contract to produce her
theatre publicity. In *Gismonda*, Bernhardt's character was set
against a background of Byzantine-style mosaics. The text font
in serpentine lettering became typical of Mucha's work. The
Gismonda poster would make Mucha the talk of Paris; his
decorative form of Art Nouveau would become *Le Style Mucha*,
all made famous because of Bernhardt. By 1896 Mucha had
become the graphic artist everyone wanted to employ; advertisers
wanted him to create advertisements for every product from
wines and chocolates to train travel and holiday resorts. The
full-length format used by Mucha proved popular with artists,
advertisers and printers.

Costumes and Jewellery

The success of the new poster for Bernhardt was not only
attributable to its elongated shape or the depiction of its star,
the 'Divine Sarah'. It was the decorative detail that Mucha had
added to her costumes and her hair that was so desirable. She
looked fabulous and each new poster only added to her glamour.
The jewellery she wore, depicted by Mucha, was much admired.
Pieces were made especially for her and other women wanted
jewellery in this Art Nouveau style, too; pieces such as the
emerald-green *Pendant brooch designed as two dragonflies*,

c. 1895–1900 (*see* page 89), made by René Lalique (1860–1945) were in demand. Commercial jewellers, recognizing a trend, joined in the craze, mass-producing cheaper copies to fill public demand. Mucha began to design some of the jewellery and costumes for Bernhardt, which in turn directly led to a commission from the jeweller Georges Fouquet (1862–1957) to create glamorous pieces for his Paris shop.

The 'Mucha Woman'

The decorative style of posters produced for Bernhardt was a formulation of many strands of Mucha's previous work, firstly as a theatrical-set painter, followed by his work as a mural painter and also portrait artist. Earlier, in 1892, Mucha had been commissioned to produce lithographs for an in-house calendar for Champenois. It was a decorative *Zodiac* series. *La Plume* magazine chose it for an in-house calendar, too. Here, one can see how Mucha's decorative design captured the spirit of an Art Nouveau that publishers wanted to associate with their products. The *Zodiac* lithograph was published again in 1896 (*see* pages 90–91), and it fully illustrates what was so different about Mucha's work. The *Zodiac* is work that captured the *Zeitgeist* of the last years of the nineteenth century. The young female typifies the style that would become the trademark 'Mucha woman'. She was a sexual amalgam of virgin, temptress, goddess and peasant. Her long hair is styled in 'macaroni' or 'noodle' waves, intricately woven into the decorative pattern of the picture. The highly stylized image is full of Symbolism, connoting the astrological zodiac. The hair and the circular patterns within the frame closely resemble the sinuous 'whiplash' lines used by the Belgian designer Victor Horta (1861–1947). Lines that Horta employed as decorative

Alphonse Mucha
Job (cigarette box), 1896
© Mucha Trust 2009

MEDIUM: unknown

RELATED WORKS: Jules Chéret,
Poster for *Job, papier a cigarettes*, 1889

Alphonse Mucha
Poster for *Job*, 1898
© Mucha Trust 2009

MEDIUM: Lithograph

RELATED WORKS: Will True (b. 1866),
Caricature of *Alphonse Mucha* for
The Poster magazine, 1898

IMP. F. CHAMPENOIS, 66.Boul? St Michel, PARIS.

detail in his wrought-iron bannisters and wall art in two innovative houses in Brussels: *Hôtel Tassel*, 1893 and *Hôtel Sôlvay*, 1894 (*see* page 91). It shows how European artists continuously transferred techniques, articulating Art Nouveau in architecture, interior design, painting and graphic art.

Le Style Mucha

The style of the young 'Mucha woman' model in the *Zodiac* lithograph reappears in several forms of advertising, all created by Mucha for clients wishing to tap into his popular poster style, and utilized to promote and symbolize aspects of modern life. His *Monaco-Monte-Carlo* poster of 1897 (*see* pages 92–93) was originally created as an advertisement for the newly opened railway line, encouraging tourists to venture to Monaco, via rail. Mucha depicts a young woman with Monte Carlo in the background and the iconic casino clearly visible. To the right and behind are the Alps.

Mucha created this Art Nouveau poster using the organic forms that included plant motifs and wildlife. In this version of the poster, produced as a limited-edition lithograph, the railway company's name and fare details have been removed. Another example is a successful campaign that resulted from Mucha's publicity for Job cigarette papers; a brand name developed in 1834 by a man called Jean Bardou (1799–1852), from his initials 'J' and 'B'. The 'O' is often stylized so that Bardou's initials are the dominant focus. In *Job*, 1898 (*see* page 95), there is repetition of the company's logo with the lozenge shaped 'O' in the background. The logo also reappears in the brooch being worn by the model, making the link between the product and the consumer. The advertisements were primarily aimed at the new market for women smokers who until this time were barred from smoking in public because of social mores.

Decorative Panneaux

In 1896 Mucha produced the first of a series of 'seasons'
panels, using four different poses of scantily clad women in an
appropriate setting for each. The following year he repeated the
exercise but used a longer panel, similar to the format employed
in the *Gismonda* poster for Sarah Bernhardt (*see* pages 88–89). The
panels were more intricate, full of pattern, Symbolism and Mucha
Style. Each 'season' was symbolized by a female surrounded by
the season's attributes. The four *Season panels,* 1900 (*see* pages
96–99), were intended to be reproduced as calendars, postcards

and menu cards, but Mucha's
publisher Champenois suggested
that the designs lent themselves
well to *panneaux.* These designs
were transferred on to silk or
fine handmade papers and framed
to resemble oriental panels. Like
many artists of his generation,
Mucha was influenced by the
surge of Japanese prints
available in Europe.

1900

Mucha's last series of 'seasons'
was completed in 1900 specifically
for *panneaux,* which were popular
in Europe at the time and used
as screens and wall decorations.
These are the most detailed of

all the series. Spring is sensuous, the swirling lines of her lower dress balancing the curved line of her right hip that creates movement. This is accentuated by the confines of the long narrow panel shape. The organic forms of the stylized plants, particularly those used in the top corner of the panel, are redolent of the designs of Horta and Hector Guimard (1867–1942). Likewise, the summer figure is a symbol of abundance, the image adorned with many flowers and the border more dramatically Art Nouveau in style. By contrast, the autumn figure is reflective and demure, although the organic forms in the corners are more

pronounced in this panel. The woman's costume and headdress is distinctly non-western European and is perhaps a Slavic motif from Mucha's homeland. In the winter image, Mucha used heavy delineation in some of the outlines, particularly around the stylized snow, resembling the images of the early nineteenth-century Japanese artist Utagawa (Andō) Hiroshige (1797–1858). Mucha expanded the motif further by suggesting that the model is wearing a kimono-style costume.

The artist has resisted the temptation of decorating the garment, preferring instead the *yukata*, a very plain style of kimono that emphasizes the spirit of the season when

Alphonse Mucha
The Seasons: Autumn, 1900
© Mucha Trust 2009

MEDIUM: Lithograph

RELATED WORKS: Dante Gabriel
Rossetti (1828–82), *Venus Verticordia*, 1864–68

Alphonse Mucha
The Seasons: Winter, 1900
© Mucha Trust 2009

MEDIUM: Lithograph

RELATED WORKS: Margaret
MacDonald Mackintosh, *Ill Omen*, 1893

there is little foliage or colour, the model's face providing the only warmth and colour to the scene. The organic pattern forms are also more restricted in this panel, especially in the corners.

Mucha Mania: from Europe to USA

Alphonse Mucha always sought to make art popular and founded, with other Art Nouveau practitioners, including Lalique and Horta, the *Société Internationale de l'Art Populaire* in 1898. His style, intrinsically linked to other contemporary practitioners of Art Nouveau, owed much to the iconography of his Slavic heritage, mixed with the characteristics of Byzantine

art. His female figures accentuated their femininity and sexuality – most particularly in the flamboyant costumes, dramatic floral motifs and curving lines – to create women who were more mystical than realistic. His delicate patterning and use of line served as a hallmark for the Art Nouveau style. Despite the essentially French themes, his work always maintained links with his Slavic origins. In the first decade of the twentieth century, interest in Art Nouveau had peaked in Europe and from 1904 Mucha began to work for American clients. For short periods, from 1905 to 1910, he lived in America with his wife, nurturing new commissions.

Alphonse Mucha *(overleaf)*
Ivy **(detail), 1901**
© Mucha Trust 2009

MEDIUM: Lithograph

RELATED WORKS: Alphonse Mucha,
Têtes Byzantines: Brunette, 1897

Alphonse Mucha *(overleaf)*
Laurel **(detail), 1901**
© Mucha Trust 2009

MEDIUM: Lithograph

RELATED WORKS: Alphonse Mucha,
Têtes Byzantines: Blonde, 1897

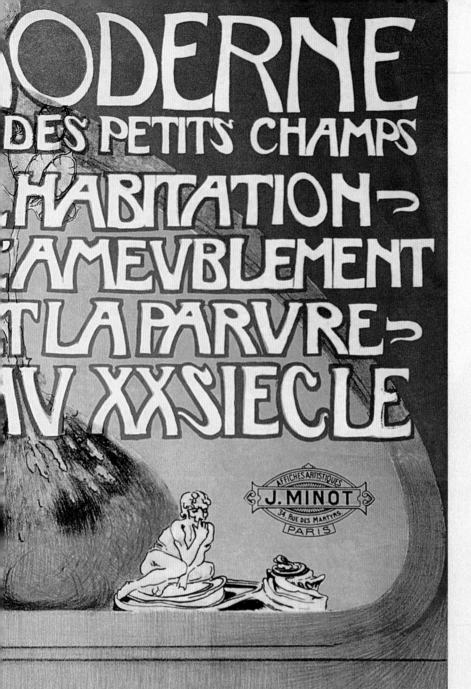

EMMANUEL ORAZI (1860–1934)

Art and Symbolism

Emmanuel (Manuel) Orazi (1860–1934) was born in Rome
but moved to Paris to work as an illustrator in 1892. He illustrated
a number of novels and worked for several magazines. His early
watercolours were reproduced as engravings. In 1895 he produced
a series of Symbolist illustrations for *Calendrier Magique*, published
1896, by Austin de Croze (active 1890s). It was a limited edition
of 777 copies, dedicated to the occult. It shows Orazi's work as a
magical diffusion of art and Symbolism. In 1899 he began working
as a designer for La Maison Moderne, an emporium of furniture,
decorative and fine art, competing with Siegfried (a.k.a. Samuel)
Bing's (1838–1905) store L'Art Nouveau; Julius Meier-Graefe
(1867–1935) opened La Maison Moderne to promote different
forms of European Art Nouveau. Orazi designed jewellery for the
store but is remembered for his stunning poster *La Maison Moderne*,
c. 1902 (*see* left), which reflects this diversity of Art Nouveau to
create a chic, aesthetically modern direction for the new century.
The sinuous form of the elegant model in profile complements
the curved chair, which is redolent of the designs of the Belgian
Henry van de Velde (1863–1957) and of the German Bruno Paul
(1874–1968). Orazi's draughtsmanship is perfect, enabling the
viewer to see in detail many of the objects on sale.

Portrait of an Era

Orazi, like many other artists in Paris, was employed in the
promotion of the world of theatre and café-concert, through
publicity posters. In 1891, he had depicted the actress Sarah
Bernhardt as Theodora, the Byzantine empress, in a scene from
the play of the same name, using an elaborate mosaic pattern

Emmanuel Orazi
Poster for *La Maison Moderne*, *c.* 1902
© Musée des Arts Décoratifs, Paris,
France/The Bridgeman Art Library

MEDIUM: unknown

RELATED WORKS: Aubrey Beardsley,
Poster for *Singer Pianos*, 1890s

to reflect the setting. However, in *Portrait of Sarah Bernhardt*, *c.* 1890s (*see* left), she is seen as herself, without theatricality. Orazi updated the background to reflect the Art Nouveau style prevalent at the time. Bernhardt is contemplative; the shape of her body is accentuated by her costume. On her belt and sleeves are organic patterns that break the simplicity of her clothes. The highly stylized and irregular plant forms, in keeping with the Art Nouveau mode, dominate the background. Most notably, Orazi has highlighted Bernhardt's frizzed red hair and pale complexion in a non-idealized manner. He, as did many others of the period, considered her to be 'The Divine Sarah'.

Emmanuel Orazi
Portrait of Sarah Bernhardt
(detail), *c.* **1890s**
© Ferrers Gallery, London, UK/
The Bridgeman Art Library

MEDIUM: unknown

RELATED WORKS: Alphonse Mucha,
Poster for *Gismonda*, 1894

Georges de Feure
Poster for *Le Journal des Ventes*, **1897**
Courtesy of Private Collection/The Stapleton
Collection/The Bridgeman Art Library/
© DACS 2009

MEDIUM: Lithograph

RELATED WORKS: Koloman Moser,
Poster for *Frommes Calendar*, 1902

GEORGES DE FEURE
(1868–1943)

La Plume

Georges Joseph de Sluiters (1868–1943) adopted his French name after moving to Paris from Holland in 1890. The son of an architect, he initially trained and worked with Chéret on his interior designs for Le Chat Noir amongst other work. As did several artists of the Art Nouveau period, De Feure executed illustrations for *La Plume*, an arts and literary magazine first published in 1889. This popular magazine was founded and run by Léon Deschamps (1860–1913), a poet who encouraged other great literary talents such as Paul Verlaine (1844–96) and Stéphane (Étienne) Mallarmé (1842–98) to contribute. Deschamps also encouraged many of the illustrators and Symbolist artists such as Denis and Gauguin to provide artwork and he set up the *Salon des Cent*, a monthly exhibition of graphic arts, which was very popular between 1890 and 1899 and included works by Mucha, Steinlen and of course De Feure. In 1894 De Feure created a poster to promote the *Fifth Exhibition of the Salon des Cent*, (*see* page 106); it is a work that pays homage to the Pre-Raphaelite artists, particularly Dante Gabriel Rossetti (1828–82), as well as to his contemporaries, particularly Manet and Degas, who often depicted solitary female figures in a café setting. De Feure's use of colour and stylization make the poster typically Art Nouveau and it shares a similar aesthetic to that of Toulouse-Lautrec.

ENTRÉE

o,50cts

5me EXPOSITION
du 1er au 31 Octobre

SALON DES CENT · 31· Rue Bonaparte.

Imp. BOURGERIE & CIE, 83, Faubg St Denis. Paris.

Symbolism

De Feure was also drawn to Symbolism as an influence for his art, probably from his exposure to other artists such as Denis, Gauguin and Odilon Redon (1840–1916) at the *Salon des Cent*. Originally a literary movement, Symbolism was adopted by a number of artists seeking a more spiritual dimension to their work. The writer Albert Aurier (1865–92) defined it as 'the painting of ideas'. It was a rejection of Naturalism and Realism in favour of a more mystical approach to art, emphasizing the depiction of sensations and emotions. There were important precursors to the movement, for example in the paintings of the Pre-Raphaelites, but it was Gauguin who gave the movement its impetus by insisting that the emotional response to nature was more significant than the purely visual. De Feure's depiction of *Joan of Arc*, 1896 (*see* right), demonstrates this idea. An idealized woman has replaced the iconography of Joan (*c.* 1412–31), the fifteenth-century warrior, who dressed as a man. This suggests a preoccupation with another aspect of Symbolism – the notion of the *femme fatale* who made many appearances in Symbolist art. Capturing the essence of the female spirit, albeit from a male perspective, became something of a trademark for De Feure. In this work he has given Joan lilac gauntlets rather than the archetypal silver armour, highlighting her femininity, as underpinned by the lettering of her name. It is also interesting to note that De Feure suggests her sainthood, with paintwork resembling a nimbus, even though she was not canonized until the twentieth century, many years after his work. The design was executed for a drapery store that was promoting a particular style of couture aimed at the modern emancipated young woman.

Georges de Feure
Poster for *the Fifth Exhibition of the Salon des Cent*, 1894
Courtesy of Private Collection/The Stapleton Collection/The Bridgeman Art Library/ © DACS 2009

MEDIUM: Lithograph

RELATED WORKS: Henri de Toulouse-Lautrec, Poster for *Le Divan Japonais*, 1892

Georges de Feure
Poster for *Joan of Arc Costumes*, 1896
Courtesy of Private Collection/The Stapleton Collection/The Bridgeman Art Library/ © DACS 2009

MEDIUM: Lithograph

RELATED WORKS: Gustav Klimt, *Nuda Veritas*, 1899

De Feure, pinx.   Typogravure Goupil, Paris.

INTÉRIEUR MODERNE (A.D.)

1900

Siegfried Bing

De Feure was one of the most-prolific designers of the Art Nouveau period despite his lack of formal training. His disciplines included not just graphics, but also interiors, furniture and *objets d'art*. He even held the post of professor of decorative arts at the École des Beaux-Arts in the 1890s. It was, however, his work for Bing, who had opened his gallery La Maison de l'Art Nouveau in 1895, that provided his main income. Bing had seen the artist's work at the *Salon des Cent* and commissioned him to make furniture and *objets d'art* such as ceramics for his gallery. He quickly became one of Bing's top designers as well as developing his own design practice and clientele. It is likely that De Feure used a number of furniture designers in his practice, such as Louis Majorelle (1859–1926), who is normally associated with Art Nouveau developments in Nancy rather than Paris, alongside Emile Gallé (1846–1904). De Feure gives us a sense of his

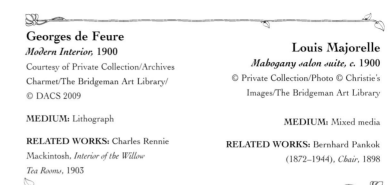

Georges de Feure
Modern Interior, 1900
Courtesy of Private Collection/Archives
Charmet/The Bridgeman Art Library/
© DACS 2009

MEDIUM: Lithograph

RELATED WORKS: Charles Rennie
Mackintosh, *Interior of the Willow
Tea Rooms,* 1903

Louis Majorelle
Mahogany salon suite, c. 1900
© Private Collection/Photo © Christie's
Images/The Bridgeman Art Library

MEDIUM: Mixed media

RELATED WORKS: Bernhard Pankok
(1872–1944), *Chair,* 1898

interiors in his poster called *Modern Interior*, 1900 (*see* left). In this same year he designed a number of room sets for Bing for his Pavilion Bing at the *Exposition Universelle*. For that he designed a boudoir that used sinuous and sensuous lines to provide an elegant space for a woman. He also designed furniture with intricate marquetry, not dissimilar to Majorelle's *Mahogany salon suite, c.* 1900 (*see* below), and carpets for the scheme.

EUGÈNE GRASSET
(1841–1917)

Maîtres de l'Affiche

After arriving in Paris in 1871 from his formal art training in Switzerland where he was born, Eugène Grasset (1841–1917) began working as a painter and sculptor before designing fabrics, ceramics and jewellery. It is some of these designs, made in the late 1870s, that seem to anticipate the Art Nouveau style. Having helped in the design of fabrics for the Chat Noir club in the 1880s, Grasset came into contact with many of the avant-garde artists later associated with the Art Nouveau style, including Steinlen and Toulouse-Lautrec. At this time, and heavily influenced by Japanese wood-block prints, Grasset began making posters becoming one of the so-called *Maîtres de l'Affiche* (masters of

Philippe Wolfers
Centrepiece, c. 1900
© Christie's Images Ltd, 2009

MEDIUM: Metal with enamel plaques

RELATED WORKS: C.R. Ashbee
(1863–1942), *Bowl*, 1892

Eugène Grasset
Poster for *Grasset Exhibition at the*
Salon des Cent, date unknown
© Private Collection/The Stapleton
Collection/The Bridgeman Art Library

MEDIUM: Lithograph

RELATED WORKS: Alphonse Mucha,
Poster for *La Dame aux Camélias*, 1896

MAI

MAY

the poster). These designs came to the attention of the American market including *Harper's Bazaar* magazine, who commissioned Grasset to illustrate the cover of their December 1894 issue. This and other Grasset work for other American magazines helped to create the market there for the Art Nouveau style.

Bringing Ideas Together

The simple design Grasset used in the poster for his own *Exhibition at the Salon des Cent* (*see* pages 110–11), demonstrates another aspect of his work: the stained-glass designs he executed for Louis Comfort Tiffany (1848–1933). The image is considerably less dramatic than many of his other designs of women, such as his *La Vitrioleuse* (the acid thrower), 1894. Both of these images are, however, clearly indebted to Japanese woodcut prints in their lack of perspective, simple and emboldened line and reduced use of colour. The use of translucent glass in Art Nouveau *objets d'art* can also be seen in Philippe Wolfers' (1858–1929) *Centrepiece, c.* 1900 (*see* page 110), which is redolent of the Arts and Crafts work of C.R. Ashbee (1863–1942), an aesthetic widely appreciated in Europe through Britain's *The Studio* magazine. Grasset was an important interpreter of the English Arts and Crafts style in France and was for a while professor of decorative arts at the École Normale d'Enseignement de Dessin in Paris. He also seemed to bring together the ideas of the Nabis painters with the craft of *cloisonné* in his graphic designs, and also designed stained glass and enamelled jewellery himself.

Department Stores

In 1894 Grasset was commissioned by the La Belle Jardinière department store to design a calendar. In the last quarter of the nineteenth century a number of large such department stores had opened in Paris selling clothes, furniture, home accessories and *objets d'art*. Many artists of the time responded to the market and began designing products for the bourgeoisie. Most of the stores were based on the affluent right bank of the Seine. Grasset's calendar creation, a page of which is shown on the left was printed

Eugène Grasset
May, page from a calendar,
date unknown
© Private Collection/The Bridgeman
Art Library

MEDIUM: unknown

RELATED WORKS: Kate Greenaway
(1846–1901), *Tea Party, c.* 1880

as high-quality chromolithographs and such was the quality of the work that the poet and writer Léon Bloy (1846–1917) wrote about them in a very poetical way, describing them as akin to the highest-quality Renaissance religious iconography.

At the *Exposition Universelle* in 1900, Grasset launched his own typeface, which he incorporated in some of his later designs. He also became a teacher of design at the École Estienne in Paris and was a founding member of the *Société des Artistes Décorateurs* in 1901, responsible for internationally disseminating design ideas. Although the group was not particularly influential outside of France, it was responsible for organizing the *Exposition Internationale des Arts Décoratifs et Industriels Modernes* in Paris in 1925, an exhibition that would promote the Art Deco style.

PAUL BERTHON
(1872–1909)

Chromolithography

Paul Emile Berthon (1872–1909) studied painting before moving to Paris in 1893 and becoming a pupil of Eugène Grasset, the professor of decorative arts at the École Normale d'Enseignement de Dessin. His main output was in large coloured posters in the relatively new medium of chromolithography, some of which were printed under the direction of Jules Chéret by Chaix

& Company. The chromolithographs facilitated the rendering of more accurate reproductions of an original painting and the ability to enhance colour if appropriate, making it an ideal medium for poster work.

Portraying the Femme Fatale

Berthon became well known for his Art Nouveau portrayals of the *femme fatale*, an altogether different interpretation of women from those of either Grasset or Chéret. His images seem to be borrowed from the Pre-Raphaelites with the heavy eyelids, pale complexion and long copper-coloured hair. For example, his 1897 poster for *L'Ermitage* (*see* left and right), an arts review magazine, is redolent of Rossetti's *Portrait of Elizabeth Siddal*, 1854, and John Waterhouse's (1849–1917) image of *Ophelia*, *c.* 1894, which is contemporary with Berthon's. Many of these Pre-Raphaelite images would have been familiar to Berthon, since they were exhibited at the *Exposition Universelles* of 1878 and 1889. The artist shows the figure in the *L'Ermitage* poster as chaste, suggested by the plethora of lilies symbolizing purity. The fleur-de-lys symbol in the top right may be a response to the writer Octave Mirbeau (1848–1917) who in 1895 called for artists to eschew French imitation of Pre-Raphaelitism in an article called 'Des lys! Des lys!'.

Multicultural Motifs

The chasteness of Berthon's *L'Ermitage* poster is in great contrast with one for Liane de Pougy (1869–1950), a celebrated dancer and infamous courtesan, which he produced to promote her appearance at the Folies-Bergère – *Liane de Pougy at the Folies-Bergère*, *c.* 1890s (*see* page 116). He depicts her as a *femme fatale* drawing her 'victim' into the spider's web to be devoured at her pleasure.

Paul Berthon
Poster for *L'Ermitage*, 1897
© Plaket Museum, Essen, Germany/
The Bridgeman Art Library

MEDIUM: Lithograph

RELATED WORKS: Evelyn de Morgan
(1855–1919), *Hero Holding the Beacon for
Leander*, 1885

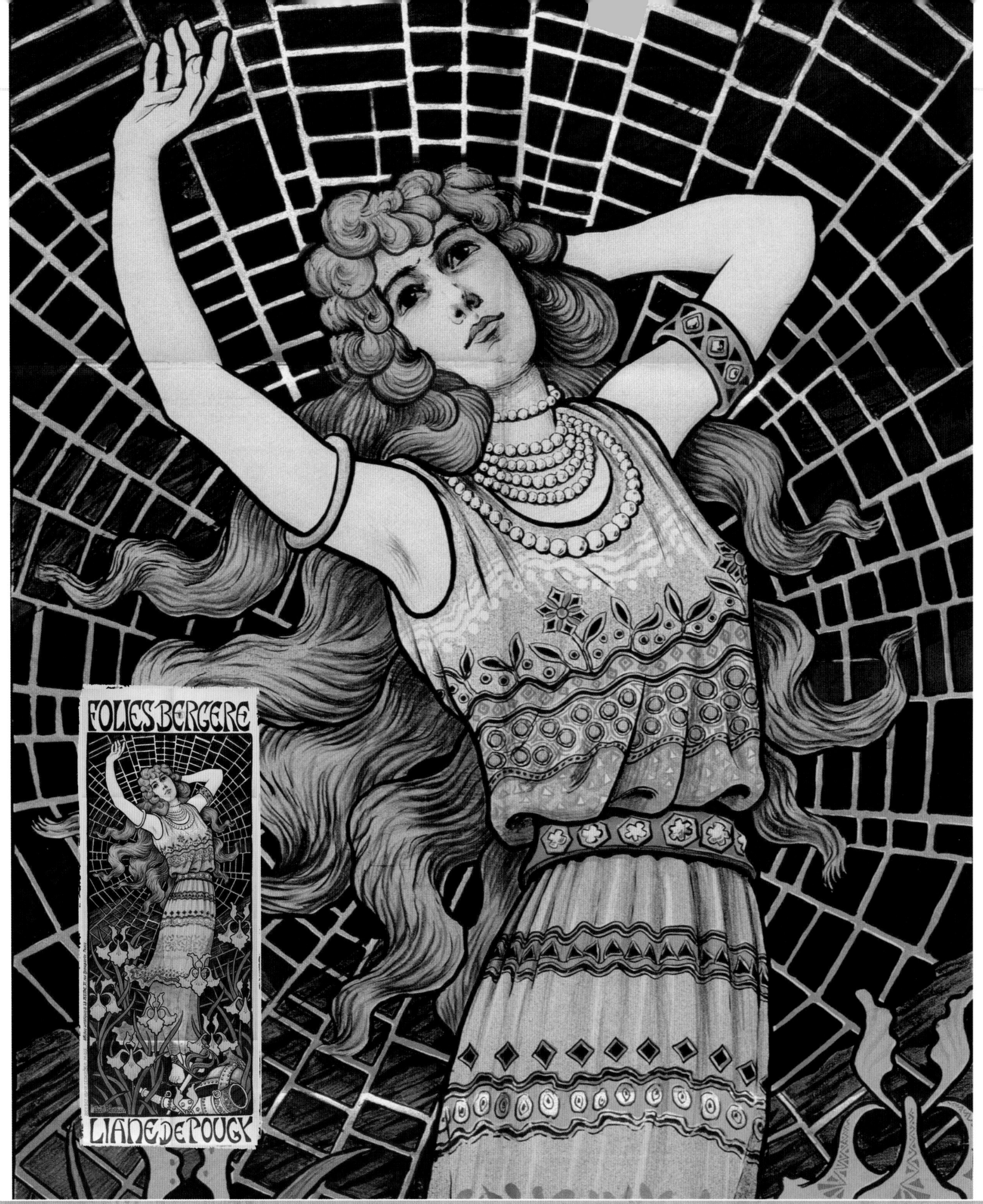
FOLIES BERGERE
LIANE DE POUGY

The commonalities in the two women are their lithesome figures and the wearing of an arm bangle, a fashion accessory of the period. The Art Nouveau period often appropriated motifs from other cultures, this being Indian. In a similar way, Lalique used the cobra and other multicultural motifs in his jewelry designs, as shown in his *Coiled snake pendant*, 1898–99 (*see* right). The serpentine style of the work is synonymous with the Art Nouveau aesthetic, and yet jewellery such as this rarely makes an appearance in contemporary posters of the time.

Master Craftsman

Berthon was a master of his craft and understood well how to adapt his style to the chromolithograph poster. The image for his *L'Ermitage* poster was selected by Jules Chéret to be included in his *Les Maîtres de l'Affiche*, an almanac of the very best in poster design, which contains 256 lithographs by many of the finest practitioners of poster art. The subscribers to *Les Maîtres* were pan-European and American, ensuring that the artwork had a very wide audience and appreciation. Berthon also produced bindings for books, which he exhibited at the official Paris Salon in 1895 together with some of his furniture designs. He also designed ceramics for Villeroy and Boch, one of the leading European porcelain makers of the time, yet it is his poster work for which he is renowned, work that borrowed from Pre-Raphaelitism, but which was heavily imbued with French Symbolism. His images were used in literary magazines such as *La Plume* and he also illustrated the cover for the *Salon des Cent* exhibition catalogue. Unfortunately Berthon died at the young age of 37 before we could witness his maturity in the Art Deco period.

Paul Berthon
*Poster for Liane de Pougy
at the Folies-Bergère, c. 1890s*
© Private Collection/Archives Charmet/
The Bridgeman Art Library

MEDIUM: Lithograph

RELATED WORKS: Walter Crane,
*Cartoon for stained-glass window
at Walthamstow*, 1880s

René Lalique
*Coiled snake pendant with
chain, 1898–99*
Courtesy of Hermitage, St Petersburg,
Russia/The Bridgeman Art Library/
© ADAGP, Paris and DACS, London 2009

MEDIUM: Gold, pearls and
champlevé enamel

RELATED WORKS: Henry van de Velde,
Pendants, 1900

HENRI PRIVAT-LIVEMONT
(1861–1936)

Art Nouveau Excellence

A near contemporary of Mucha, Henri Privat-Livemont (1861–1936) shared a similar aesthetic with his Czech counterpart, both of whom absorbed the style of Eugène Grasset, before taking it to a higher level of superb draughtsmanship and Art Nouveau excellence. Livemont was born in Schaerbeek, Brussels, and trained initially at the École des Arts Décoratifs as an interior decorator before taking up a scholarship to study in Paris from 1883. Whilst there he executed a number of stage-set designs, decorating them himself while studying in the evenings at the École Estienne. He later returned to Brussels to begin his long career as a poster artist, lithographer and printmaker.

Poster Design

The Scent of a Rose, c. 1890 (*see* right), is an early Livemont poster that clearly shows his talent for colour and design. It incorporates the 'whiplash' lines synonymous with Art Nouveau, particularly the Belgian interpretation of the style, and its decorative language found a resonance with a number of applied artists, such as the French ceramicist (Pierre) Adrien Dalpayrat (1844–1910), whose design for an earthenware *Vase* (*see* left) clearly pays deference.

(Pierre) Adrien Dalpayrat	**Henri Privat-Livemont**
Vase, date unknown	*The Scent of a Rose*, c. 1890
© Private Collection/Photo © Christie's Images/The Bridgeman Art Library	© Private Collection/Photo © Christie's Images/The Bridgeman Art Library
MEDIUM: Earthenware	**MEDIUM:** unknown
RELATED WORKS: Bernard Cuzner (1877–1956), *Silver bowl, c.* 1906	**RELATED WORKS:** Alejandro de Riquer (1856–1920), Poster for *Joventut*, 1900

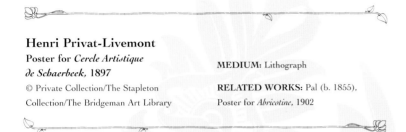

Henri Privat-Livemont
Poster for *Cercle Artistique
de Schaerbeek*, 1897
© Private Collection/The Stapleton
Collection/The Bridgeman Art Library

MEDIUM: Lithograph

RELATED WORKS: Pal (b. 1855),
Poster for *Abricotine*, 1902

Unlike some of his contemporaries, Livemont portrayed his women
as languid rather than as *femmes fatales*. In *The Scent of a Rose* his
style is rather peculiar in that he not only adopted the Japanese-
influenced heavy delineation of form, but also created a white
parallel border to the black line to create a seemingly cut-out figure.
The style of the poster is totally Art Nouveau with the sinuous
forms at the top and the overlapping use of flowers and plants
on the portrait's frame. The woman is, however, rather anonymous
and without individual personality, and this is emphasized by her
particularly abstract tendril-like hair. In many ways the images
are redolent of his contemporary Mucha, but Livemont used much
stronger colours and contrasts, and his later work was less frivolous
and tended to embrace aspects of Symbolism. His use of roses has
strong links to both pagan and Christian tradition, as exemplified
by many of the Renaissance artists.

Cercle Artistique de Schaerbeek

Livemont began to develop his work along more Symbolist
lines in the mid-1890s. He was one of the founding members of
the *Cercle Artistique de Schaerbeek*, which was set up to exhibit art
and design in Brussels and to enlighten the Belgians of the new
style. His poster from 1897 for the fifth exhibition of the group
(*see* left and right) depicts a young woman in a narcissistic pose;
narcissism was an aspect of human behaviour that was of interest
to writers and artists, most notably Oscar Wilde (1854–1900)
in his 1890 novel *The Picture of Dorian Gray*. Artists under the
umbrella of Symbolism were also drawn to the phenomenon,
for example Edward Burne-Jones's (1833–98) *The Baleful Head*,
c. 1876. The 'new art' appealed to many Belgians still trying to
throw off the vestiges of their country's French past and so create
a new and independent identity. The King of Belgium, Leopold II

(1835–1909), also known as the 'builder' king, was only the
second monarch to rule since their independence from France
in 1830, but was still using the *Beaux-Arts* style of architecture.
In contrast, the newly emerging Belgian Workers' Party,
supported by the country's intellectuals, railed against this style
and sought to encourage young designers such as Horta to create
the new public buildings such as the *Maison du Peuple*, 1895–99,
advocating a more modern and independent form of architecture
– the emerging Art Nouveau. So too did artists such as Livemont,
Henri Meunier (1873–1922) and Victor Mignot (1872–1944) aim
to find new modes of expression for new ideas.

Henri Privat-Livemont
Poster for *Cacao van Houten*, 1897
© Victoria & Albert Museum, London, UK/
The Bridgeman Art Library

MEDIUM: Lithograph

RELATED WORKS: The Beggarstaffs
(William Nicholson and James Pryde),
Poster for *Rowntrees Cocoa*, 1894

Henri Privat-Livemont
**Poster for the *Sixth Exhibition of the
Automobile Club de France*, 1903**
© Private Collection/DaTo Images/
The Bridgeman Art Library

MEDIUM: Lithograph

RELATED WORKS: Eugène Grasset,
Poster for *Georges Richard Cycles and
Automobiles*, 1897

Van Houten Chocolate

Coenraad Johannes van Houten (1801–87) was a Dutch
chocolate maker who in 1828 invented a process for removing the
bitter taste from cocoa (the cocoa butter) to produce what was
subsequently known as 'Dutch processed' chocolate, which could
be used to make drinking chocolate. It was, however, Coenraad's
son Casparus (1844–1901) who had a talent for marketing the
company's chocolate drink and the advertisements could be
found on trams and hoardings
all over Europe at the end of the
century. Casparus was a devotee
of the Art Nouveau style, having
a huge villa built in the *Jugendstil*
and commissioning some of
the leading artists to create
advertisements for his product.
Livemont's poster for *Cacao van
Houten*, 1897 (*see* left and right), is
redolent of those by the Symbolist
Belgian artist Fernand Khnopff
(1858–1921) who portrayed
women as either predatory *femmes
fatales* or with eyes half closed
in a dream-like trance. Livemont
seems to have been inspired
by the latter mode in his poster
for van Houten's chocolate,
his model's eyes half closed,
entranced by the intoxicating
aroma of the hot chocolate.

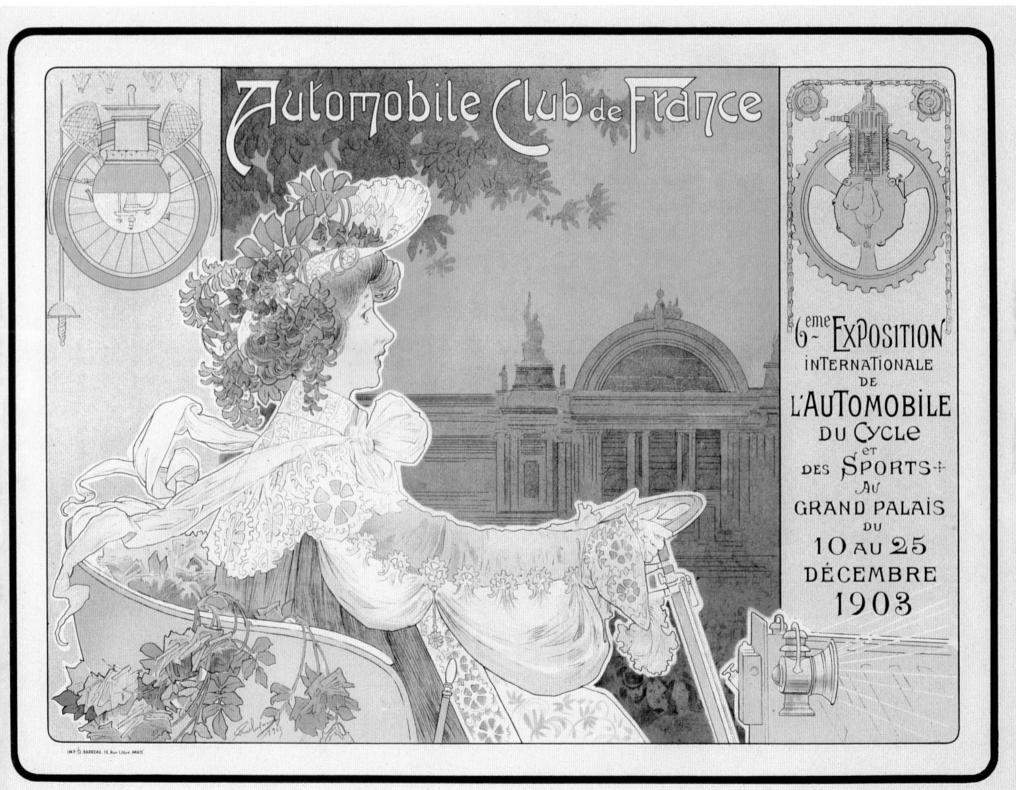

HENRI MEUNIER (1873–1922)

Early Influences

Henri Meunier came from a family of artists, including his father
Jean-Baptiste (1821–1900) and his uncle Constantin Meunier
(1831–1905), one of the most respected sculptors in Belgium.
The young Henri was, however, more interested in graphics and
printmaking. His initial training was in his home town of Ixelles,
just outside Brussels. His poster work was exhibited at Bing's
new gallery in 1896 and this brought the Belgian artist to the
attention of the dissident artists in Germany and Austria,
showing his work again with the Vienna Secessionists.

Meunier's Masterpiece

Described as his masterpiece, Meunier's poster for *Rajah*, *c.* 1897
(*see* right), is certainly one of the most iconic of all Art Nouveau
graphic designs. Its simplicity owes much to the Japanese
woodblock prints that inspired it. The palette used is limited,
enabling the viewer to consider the sinuous lines and asymmetry of
the work. It also clearly has an Egyptian influence, responding to
the increased interest in Egyptology in the late nineteenth century,
particularly in England and Continental Europe. However, its use
by Meunier is neither historical nor patronizing, and is a very
modern interpretation of an ancient culture; a European model
wearing a fashionable accessory. The image asks the viewer to
consider the supposed aroma and sensation of the coffee, in itself
a Symbolist aspiration that asks us to apply all our senses and our
mind to an aesthetic. The artist suggests that the figure depicted
is a hierarchical one, therefore making coffee, as a sensation and
deity, analogous. Meunier used different cultural motifs in his other
posters for Rajah coffee, including a Nordic theme in which the

Henri Meunier
Poster for *Rajah*, *c.* 1897
© Private Collection/The Stapleton
Collection/The Bridgeman Art Library

MEDIUM: Lithograph

RELATED WORKS: Cecil Aldin
(1870–1935), Poster for *Cadbury's Cocoa*, 1899

of the famous Belgian violinist, conductor and composer Eugène Ysaÿe (1858–1931). Ysaÿe's work was Romantic and similar in style to that of César Franck (1822–90), and the style of the poster is bold but very simple, possibly reflecting the simplicity of his and Franck's music. The image has one unusual aspect, and that includes a woman playing a double flute, an instrument not synonymous with European culture, with the possible exception of ancient Greece. The theme of motifs taken from antiquity is one that occurs many times in Symbolist art, including the use of musical instruments associated with that epoch such as the pipes and lyre, which have a romantic overtone. The image seems to have been influenced by Burne-Jones, the English Pre-Raphaelite painter who had been so successful exhibiting his work on the Continent, and who was particularly revered in Belgium. Meunier has simplified the drapery worn by Burne-Jones's models, but managed to encapsulate the spiritual Symbolism of the motif as well as the aesthetic of the serpentine rhythm of the red-haired figures. The lithesome figure suggested by Meunier is an oft-repeated motif in Art Nouveau because of its sinuous line. Koloman Moser (1868–1918) used the same idea in his *Panel from a Wiener Werkstätte single bed*, c. 1904 (*see* left). The decorations, possibly influenced by Burne-Jones's own decorative schemes, are more typical of Vienna *Secession* design.

steam from the coffee cup is used to spell out the name of the product. He also executed a number of posters for other products, most notably his *Bec Auer*, 1895, as well as creating fashion posters and the postcard designs for which he became well known.

Eugène Ysaÿe

Meunier's poster for *Ysaÿe Concerts at the Salle du Cirque Royal*, 1895 (*see* above left), advertised a series of concerts in the name

FERNAND TOUSSAINT
(1873–c. 1955)

Freehand Flair

Fernand Toussaint (1873–c. 1955) was trained in fine art in Brussels before going to Paris in 1891 to complete his education. Under the guidance of the artist Alfred Stevens (1823–1906), who specialized in portraits of elegant women, Toussaint developed his own style of fine-art Realist painting, depicting demure women in fashionable dress. He also produced delicate still-life paintings that often involved Art Nouveau interiors. Toussaint was a fine draughtsman and began producing posters from about 1895 in which elegant women usually feature. His *Café Jacqmotte*, c. 1896 (*see* right), is an advertisement

Café
Jacqmo
BRUXELLES

AFFICHES D'ART O. DE RYCKER & Cⁱᵉ BRUXELLES

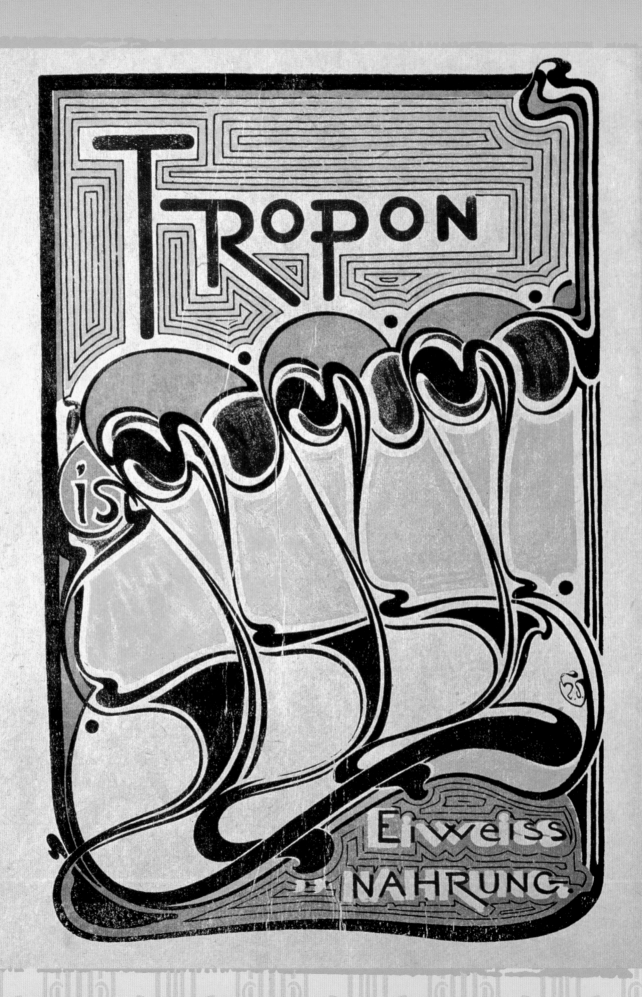

for Jacqmotte coffee houses founded in Brussels in 1828. The woman depicted is haute bourgeois, suggesting that the beverage is the preserve of the elite. However, coffee was by this time drunk by a cross section of society and even proffered by temperance movements to the working classes as an alternative beverage to alcohol. Toussaint's poster is therefore clearly aimed at the establishment serving the coffee, as a place perhaps where young unchaperoned bourgeois women could meet. The artist was renowned for the free-hand style of lettering he used in his posters, the one illustrated on page 127 being a typical example.

Henry van de Velde
Poster for *Tropon*, c. 1898
© Estate of Henry van de Velde/Private Collection/The Bridgeman Art Library

MEDIUM: Lithograph

RELATED WORKS: James Herbert MacNair and the MacDonald sisters, Poster for *The Glasgow Institute*, 1896

Henry van de Velde
***Desk and chair*, 1896**
© Estate of Henry van de Velde/ Germanisches Nationalmuseum, Nuremberg, Germany, Lauros/Giraudon/ The Bridgeman Art Library

MEDIUM: Oak

RELATED WORKS: Richard Riemerschmid (1868–1957), *Chair for a Music Room*, 1899

HENRY VAN DE VELDE
(1863–1957)

As Designer

Possibly, along with Horta, van de Velde is the most well known of all Belgian Art Nouveau practitioners. Originally he studied painting, his earliest influences being the Post-Impressionists Georges Seurat (1859–91) and Vincent van Gogh (1853–90). He also developed a friendship with the sculptor Constantin Meunier, the uncle of Henri Meunier. However, by 1892 he devoted himself to design and decoration, creating his own house *Bloemenwerf*, in 1895, very much in the British Arts and Crafts styles of Charles Voysey (1857–1941) or Mackay Baillie-Scott (1865–1945). The homage to the British was apparent in the interior too, with the use of William Morris wallpapers. Van de Velde was as much interested in the philosophy of good-design practice as in its aesthetic, and revered the writings of Morris and

John Ruskin (1819–1900). His interiors came to the attention of Bing who commissioned him to design furniture for his store in Paris, La Maison de l'Art Nouveau. Unlike many of the other Art Nouveau creatives, van de Velde designed very few posters, and only for one client, Tropon the food concentrate company. His poster for *Tropon, c.* 1898 (*see* page 128) is pure abstraction and the 'whiplash' lines used are echoed in many of his other designs including furniture (see *Desk and chair*, 1896, page 129).

As Teacher

More than any other aspect of his design output, van de Velde was renowned for his interiors and in particular his furniture, and it was he who was responsible for disseminating the 'whiplash' aesthetic to Paris. Van de Velde's work as an educator, however, is of equal significance to his practice. He began writing in 1893 and travelled to several parts of Europe disseminating his ideas and showing his designs in Germany and at The Hague Arts and Crafts exhibition in 1898. In 1902 he was appointed artistic adviser to the Grand Duke of Weimar (1818–1901) and then professor at the new school that he designed in 1904. In 1907 he became a founder member of the *Deutscher Werkbund*, which was instrumental in promoting German design and the first step towards a modern aesthetic in industrial design. Van de Velde was never at home with mass production, however, and left after an acrimonious row with its director Hermann Muthesius (1861–1927). By this time Art Nouveau's

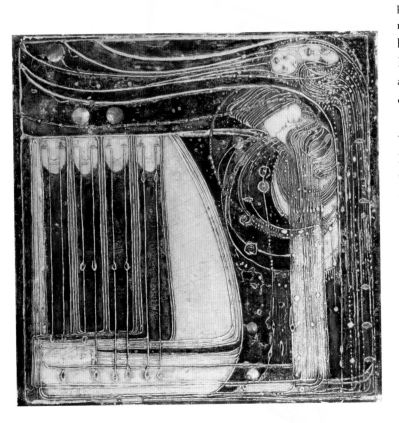

heyday was at an end and van de Velde continued to teach in Switzerland, Brussels and then as professor of architecture at the University of Ghent.

MARGARET MACDONALD MACKINTOSH (1864–1933)

A Modern Approach

Margaret and her sister Frances (1873–1921) were students at the Glasgow School of Art and it was here that they met Charles Rennie Mackintosh (1868–1928) and James Herbert MacNair (1868–1955), eventually becoming the Glasgow 'Four' and spawning the so-called Glasgow Style. Often judged unfairly as the 'decorative' contributor to her husband's more serious pursuits in architecture, Margaret Mackintosh (née MacDonald) has more recently been celebrated as a *tour de force* in design and as being influential to the Vienna Secessionists and later the *Wiener Werkstätte* in their very modern approach to design. Her graphic design for *Deutsche Kunst und Dekoration*, 1902 (*see* right), was essentially Art Nouveau, and was in fact the cover for the influential journal, which examined improved design standards in Germany. It was published between 1897 and 1933 and was at the forefront of reporting on modern design in Germany, overseeing the developments of the *Deutscher Werkbund* and of the Bauhaus. Margaret's influence was therefore at the genesis of these developments in Germany (Darmstadt and Munich) and Vienna. Her personal development, however, was as a collaborator with her husband Charles on interiors and textiles.

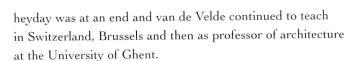

DEUTSCHE KUNST
UND DEKORATION

VERLAG
ALEX
KOCH
DARMSTADT

V. JAHRG. HEFT 8.   MAI 1902.   EINZELPREIS M. 2.⁵⁰.

CHARLES RENNIE MACKINTOSH (1868–1928)

Similarity of Style

In the early 1890s Charles Rennie Mackintosh was introduced to James Herbert MacNair and the MacDonald sisters, Margaret and Frances, by the principal of the Glasgow School of Art, where they were all studying. He had noticed the similarity in their approaches to design and encouraged them to collaborate, and from that time on they became known as the 'Glasgow Four' linking themselves both professionally and in personal relationships. Indeed it is sometimes difficult to determine exactly which of the four was responsible for a particular design, such was their similarity of style and the fact that much of the work was collaborative. The poster for *The Scottish Musical Review*, 1896 (*see* right), is by Mackintosh, but cannot be without some input from the others, however indirectly. It is an innovative design that pays little deference to its European Art Nouveau counterparts. The poster is 2 m (7 ft) high and symmetrical, which emphasizes its linearity. The typeface is unusual, incorporating vertical as well as horizontal lettering. There are references to the Celtic tradition, but its overall aesthetic and rectilinear shape pay homage to Japanese design. The style and shape of the poster was repeated a number of times by the 'Glasgow Four' and replicated a few years later by the Vienna Secessionists.

Charles Rennie Mackintosh
Poster for *The Scottish Musical Review*, 1896
© Art Gallery and Museum, Kelvingrove, Glasgow, Scotland/The Bridgeman Art Library

MEDIUM: Lithograph

RELATED WORKS: Josef Hoffmann, Poster for *The Vienna Secession Exhibition*, 1903

Charles Rennie Mackintosh
Design for a Music Room with panels by Margaret MacDonald Mackintosh, 1901
© Private Collection/The Stapleton Collection/The Bridgeman Art Library

MEDIUM: Lithograph

RELATED WORKS: Charles Rennie Mackintosh, *Bedroom for the Hill House*, 1902–03

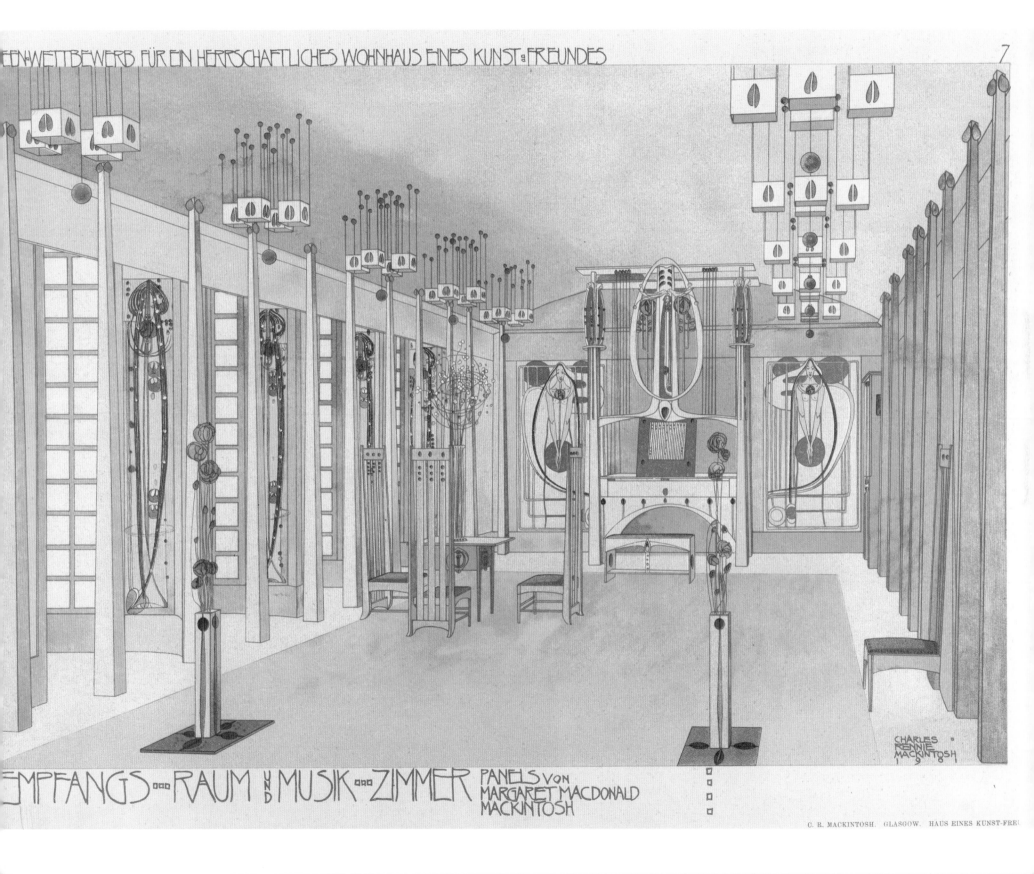

C. R. MACKINTOSH. GLASGOW. HAUS EINES KUNST-FRE

THE BEGGARSTAFFS

English Eccentricity

The Beggarstaffs were in fact brothers-in-law, William Nicholson (1872–1949) and James Pryde (1866–1941), who had both trained at the Académie Julian in Paris and been influenced by the work of Toulouse-Lautrec. Between 1893 and 1899 they collaborated on a series of graphic designs and posters that are heavily influenced by Toulouse-Lautrec but which also have a certain English eccentricity. Their most well-known work was the alphabet wood-cut series of illustrations produced for the London publisher William Heinemann and the poster for Henry Irving's (1838–1905) production of *Don Quixote* in 1895.

In many ways their poster for *Kassama Corn Flour* (*see* left) is exemplary and deserves its place among the *Maîtres de l'Affiche* collection despite its simplicity being at odds with Chéret's cheerful maidens. Its abstraction anticipates much of the aesthetic of the Modernist movement in the early years of the twentieth century, particularly in the anonymity and de-personalization of the figure. The colours are simple and bold making the viewer less likely to be distracted by her attractiveness and more likely to read the message. After the collaboration, which was not a commercial success, Nicholson resumed painting mainly still-life works in oils and Pryde became a Romantic artist, most notable for his series of paintings that he entitled *Human Comedy*, 1895–1905.

WILLIAM H. BRADLEY
(1868–1962)

American Art Nouveau

The most-famous name in American Art Nouveau is without doubt Tiffany, the aesthetic often being referred to as the Tiffany Style. However, in 1893 the Art Nouveau advertising poster came of age in America after *Harper's* produced the first of many posters to promote their magazine. Such was the quality of illustration that they were unable to meet the demand for the posters from the public. Spurred on by this success, and those of their rivals such as Scribner's, Chicago publishers Stone and Kimball commissioned Will(iam) H. Bradley to design a series of posters for their magazine, *The Chap Book*. His first one, and probably the best known, was *The Twins*, 1894, and it is generally accepted as the first Art Nouveau poster produced in America. His cover of *The Chap Book*, also 1894 (*see* right), has an equally American flavour, Thanksgiving, and also illustrates a set of twins serving up the delights of this festival. The use of a limited palette and bold sinuous lines are reminders of the Japanese influence in America as well as Europe.

The Chap Book was published over a five-year period from 1894 and helped to promote the books published by Stone and Kimball. The journal also published poetry and prose by Henry James (1843–1916), W.B. Yeats (1865–1939) and Thomas Hardy (1840–1928). Other contributors were Aubrey Beardsley (1872–98) and the caricaturist Max Beerbohm (1872–1956).

The Peacock Motif

Bradley was also commissioned by other publishers to design posters, including the influential Charles Scribner's Sons, a New York-based house responsible for publishing among others F. Scott Fitzgerald (1896–1940) and Ernest Hemingway (1899–1961). In 1895 Scribner's had published a book called

The Beggarstaffs (William Nicholson and James Pryde)
Poster for *Kassama Corn Flour,*
date unknown
© Estates of William Nicholson and James Pryde/Private Collection/The Stapleton Collection/The Bridgeman Art Library. Reproduced by permission of Elizabeth Banks

MEDIUM: Lithograph

RELATED WORKS: Cecil Aldin (1870–1935), Poster for *Colman's Blue*, 1900

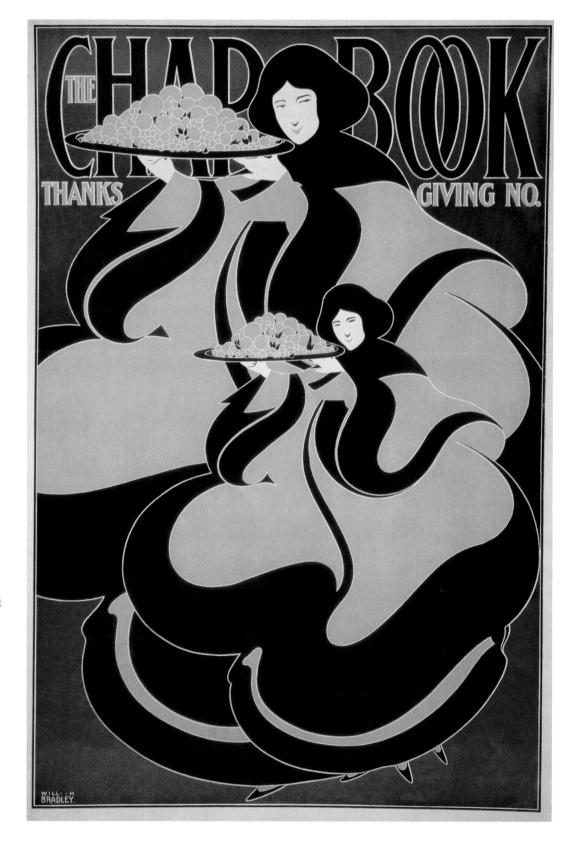

William H. Bradley
Cover of *The Chap Book*, 1894
© Estate of William H. Bradley/Victoria & Albert Museum, London, UK/ The Bridgeman Art Library

MEDIUM: Lithograph

RELATED WORKS: Victor Mignot (1872–1944), Poster for *Le Cenacle*, 1897

Tiffany Studios
(American School)
Peacock (detail), date unknown
© Private Collection/Photo © Christie's
Images/The Bridgeman Art Library

MEDIUM: Stained glass

RELATED WORKS: Gustav Klimt,
Portrait of Eugenia Primavesi, 1913–14

William H. Bradley
The Modern Poster, 1895
© Estate of William H. Bradley/Library
of Congress, Washington DC, USA/
The Bridgeman Art Library

MEDIUM: Lithograph

RELATED WORKS: Tiffany Studios
(American School), *Peacock*, date unknown

The Modern Poster, and used Bradley to design the advertising poster to promote it (*see* right). Stylistically it is very Beardsley-like in its sinuous line and restricted use of colour. However, the introduction of a peacock motif adds both pattern and colour to the design. The peacock, a Christian symbol for immortality, was popular at the end of the nineteenth century in many art objects. One example is by the Anglo-American artist James McNeill Whistler (1833–1903) who decorated a room in the London house of industrialist Frederick Leyland (1831–92) in 1876, which became known as the Peacock Room. The decoration was controversial and attracted wide publicity, which was almost certainly read by Bradley. This may well have been the influence for his design since, like Whistler, he was also interested in Japanese design. A second example

is by Tiffany who designed many objects using the motif, including his *Peacock* stained-glass window (*see* left). Shortly after Bradley created *The Modern Poster* design, he began working on his own magazine, *Bradley: His Book*, which was similar in agenda to *The Chap Book*, and continued in production until 1898.

The Bicycle Craze

The 'bicycle craze', as it became known, was a phenomenon of the 1890s both in Europe and America. It was particularly suitable as a mode of transport for independently minded women of the period. Susan Anthony, the American civil-rights campaigner for women's suffrage, went so far as to say that it was the bicycle that had emancipated women more than anything else. The effect of trying to ride a bicycle also encouraged women to seek a more emancipating form of dress, obviating the possibility of wearing full skirts. Bradley's poster for *Victor Bicycles*, 1896 (*see* below), suggests this emancipation to his audience, presumably aimed at the female market as an admiring woman oversees a female cyclist. The design is once again based on Beardsley's simple line drawings, the Art

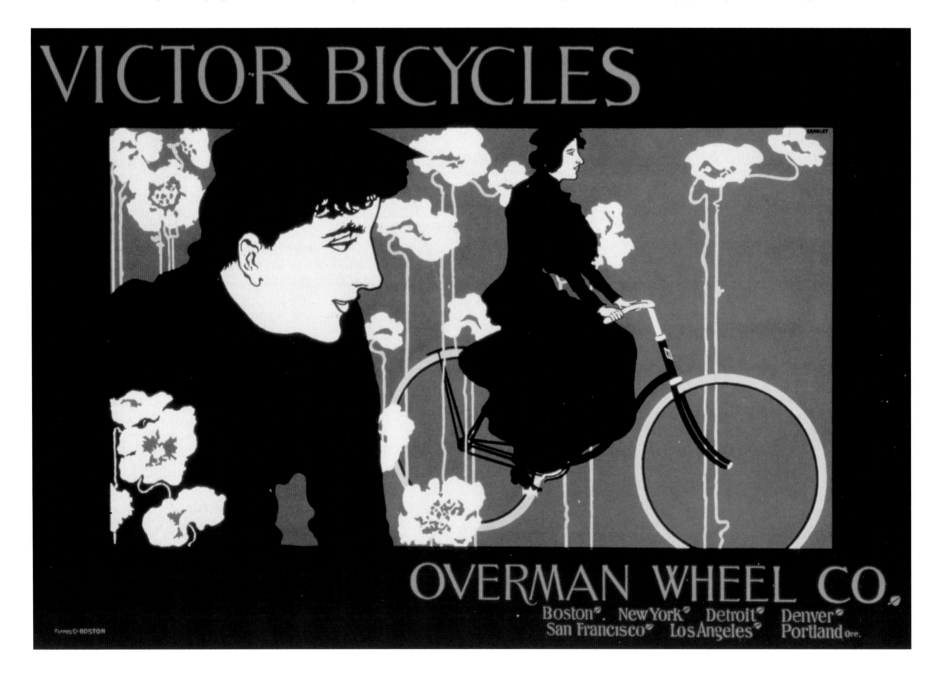

Nouveau styling added in the form of stylized flowers. The graphics used and the rectilinear shape of the design are redolent of both Margaret MacDonald Mackintosh and the *Wiener Werkstätte* artists Moser and Josef Hoffmann (1870–1956), as seen in Hoffmann's design for a *Vase*, 1910 (*see* below, right). The poster appeared in Jules Chéret's *Les Maîtres de l'Affiche* and was also used on an American commemorative postage stamp. Bradley executed other designs for Victor Bicycles in a more overt Art Nouveau style redolent of his French and Belgian counterparts, but this one is more in line with a Modernist aesthetic.

Chicago World's Fair

One of Bradley's early triumphs was the commission of a book cover, page decorations and a poster for Tom Hall's (1862–1900) book *When Hearts are Trumps*, 1894 (*see* page 140), published by Stone and Kimball in 1894. The design is once again akin to Beardsley in its sinuous line and erotic sensuality, but the figure on the left is also redolent of Rossetti's muses. He had undoubtedly been influenced by what he had seen the previous year at the World's Fair in Chicago. The fair had a profound effect on art and design in America at a time when it was beginning to show its industrial might, a power that would soon supersede European dominance, but that was still under its design influences. Ironically the fair was a celebration of Columbus's arrival in the New World 400 years before. It was the first world fair to use alternating-current electrical power to illuminate the exhibition halls, and George Ferris (1859–96) first demonstrated his wheel in the amusement park.

Bradley's Later Years

As the Art Nouveau style was waning, Bradley accepted a post as art editor for *Collier's Weekly*, which he held for three years from 1907. He was responsible for commissioning illustrators, who included Edward Penfield (1866–1925) and Edmund Dulac (1882–1953), and executed many of his own cover designs. The weekly journal was started by Peter Collier (1849–1909), an Irish immigrant, in 1888, and within four years it had achieved one of the highest circulations in America for this type of magazine.

William H. Bradley
Poster for *Victor Bicycles*, 1896
© Estate of William H. Bradley/Collection
Kharbine-Tapabor, Paris, France/
The Bridgeman Art Library

MEDIUM: Lithograph

RELATED WORKS: Alphonse Mucha,
Poster for *Waverley Cycles*, 1897

Josef Hoffmann
Vase, 1910
© Estate of Josef Hoffmann/Private
Collection/The Bridgeman Art Library

MEDIUM: White glass with black décor

RELATED WORKS: Otto Eckmann,
Stoneware vase, 1900

It was one of the earliest magazines whose remit was investigative journalism, and attracted many eminent writers such as Hemingway and even Winston Churchill (1874–1965).

Following his spell at *Collier's*, Bradley joined the staff of several magazines, most notably *Century* and *Good Housekeeping*, for both of which he designed entirely new layouts. He also wrote several short stories, gave a number of lectures and created new type fonts. He also art directed several films, independently and for the Hearst Corporation that he joined briefly in 1915, and then for a longer spell after 1921. Bradley retired in 1928 but continually worked on various projects including his autobiography, *Memories*, published in 1949. The following year he enjoyed a retrospective exhibition of his work at the prestigious Huntington Library in San Merino, California, and achieved several lifetime achievement awards from his peers. His wife of 64 years, Alice, died in 1952 and he lived for much of the rest of his own life either with his daughter, Fern, or in a rest home. He died in California at the age of 93.

LOUIS JOHN RHEAD
(1857–1926)

Aestheticism

Louis John Rhead (1857–1926) was a member of the dynastic Rhead families of potters in Stoke-on-Trent, England. In the 1870s he went to Paris to train as a painter, then returned to England and worked briefly for Cassell's the publishers in London after his art training at the National Art Training School.

While he was there he must have seen the paintings of Whistler and others of the Aesthetic movement, heavily influenced by the pervading Japanese style of the time. A feature of Aestheticism was the use of natural, often idealized, motifs that were adopted by the Art Nouveau artists later on in the century, for example the peacock. Aestheticism was, however, more than just the decorative aspects of art and applied arts. It also had a literary aspect, most notably in the writings of Oscar Wilde, adopted later by the Symbolists. The Aesthetic influence on his work is most clearly demonstrated in *Woman with Peacocks*, 1897–99 (*see* above and right), a motif used by the artists Whistler and Walter Crane (1845–1915). The image is also clearly indebted to the Nabis painter Denis in his use of a woodland setting. His model, however, is wearing the latest fashion, redolent of Grasset's posters, and demonstrates American interest in Parisian *haute couture*. Rhead's design was for a lithograph to be published by *L'Estampe Moderne* as a collectors' item.

William H. Bradley
Poster for *When Hearts are Trumps* by Tom Hall, c. 1894
© Estate of William H. Bradley/Private Collection/The Stapleton Collection/The Bridgeman Art Library

MEDIUM: Lithograph

RELATED WORKS: Joseph Sattler (1867–1931), Cover for *Pan*, 1895

Louis John Rhead
Woman with Peacocks, from *L'Estampe Moderne*, 1897–99
© Private Collection/The Stapleton Collection/The Bridgeman Art Library

MEDIUM: Lithograph

RELATED WORKS: Georges de Feure, *Retour*, 1897

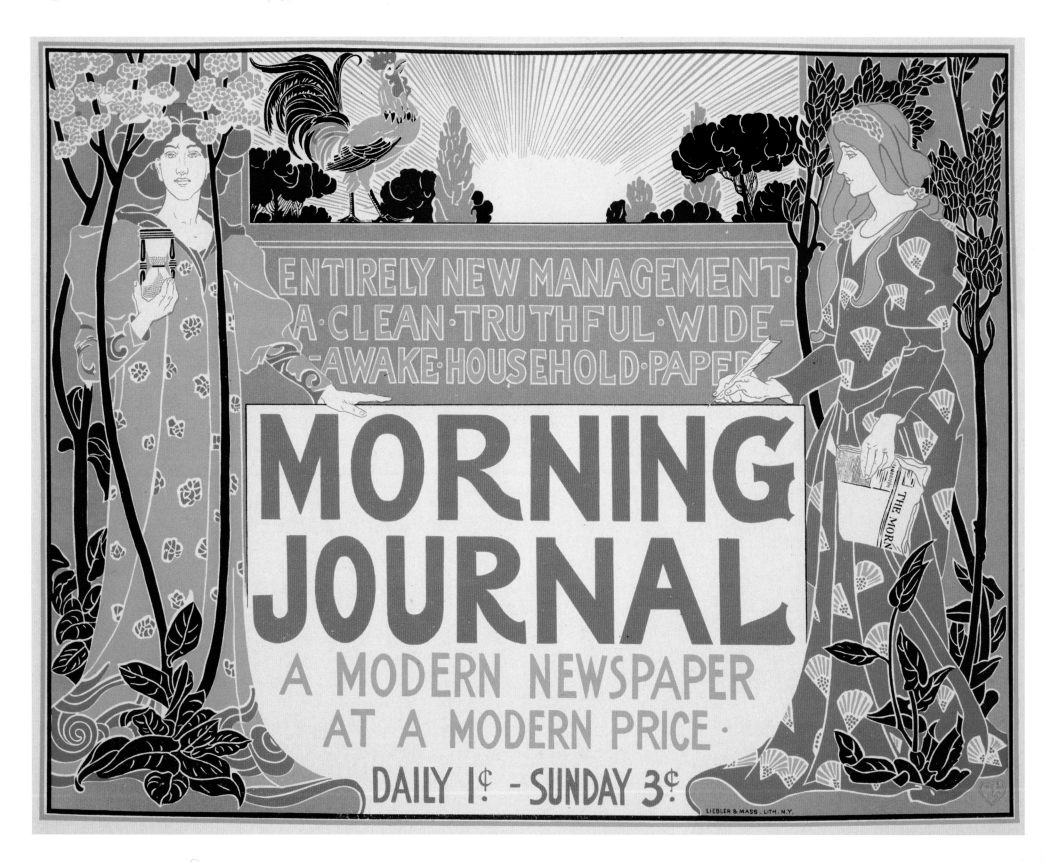

Louis John Rhead
Poster for *Morning Journal*,
date unknown
© Private Collection/The Stapleton
Collection/The Bridgeman Art Library

MEDIUM: Lithograph

RELATED WORKS: Paul-Elie Ranson,
Tristesse, 1896

Edward Penfield
Poster for *Harper's, May*, 1897
© Private Collection/The Stapleton
Collection/The Bridgeman Art Library

MEDIUM: Lithograph

RELATED WORKS: Paul Berthon,
La viole de gambe, 1899

have been Theodore Roosevelt (1858–1919), Churchill and Mark Twain (1835–1910). Penfield's first published work for *Harper's* appeared in 1891, a bold drawing that caught the attention of the art editor of the time, Frederick Schell (1838–1905). The following year he went to Paris to gain experience and on his return was perhaps surprised to learn that he was to replace Schell as art editor, to take the publication into the new age. He stayed at *Harper's* until 1901, after which he worked freelance as an illustrator. The last poster he designed for them was in August 1899. What they all have in common is the simplicity of line for which he was well known.

In America

In 1883 Rhead moved to New York to take up a post as art director for the publishers D. Appleton. The following year he married and became an American citizen. During the poster craze of the 1890s Rhead produced many designs for a wide market. In his poster for *Morning Journal* (*see* left), he borrows from the Pre-Raphaelite muse, but more heavily from the Japanese influence that was pervading art at the time. In the image, the hairstyle of the figure on the left and the kimono-style garment of the one on the right demonstrate this most clearly. Rhead probably also saw the Pre-Raphaelite influence when he was working in England in his early life. In 1895 he was presented with a gold medal for his design at the first international poster show, held in Boston. Like most graphic artists of the period, Rhead was adept at transferring his skills and illustrated a number of children's books.

EDWARD PENFIELD (1866–1925)

Designs for Harper's

A native New Yorker, Edward Penfield (1866–1925) studied painting and illustration in the city before embarking on a career with *Harper's*, firstly as an illustrator and then as art editor. Penfield joined at a time when the old woodblock processes were becoming archaic and new technologies were advancing. *Harper's* was, and still is, a general-interest magazine that was launched in America in 1850. Among its many contributors over the century and a half

Art Nouveau

Section Three

The Fine Arts

REVEALING HOW PAINTERS FROM
DISPARATE ARTISTIC BACKGROUNDS
ADOPTED ELEMENTS OF ART NOUVEAU
STYLE IN THE FINE ARTS.

THE SYNTHETISTS

In the late 1880s the French artists Paul Gauguin (1848–1903), Émile Bernard (1868–1941) and Paul Sérusier (1864–1927) were part of an artists' colony situated in and around Pont-Aven in Brittany. Gauguin was the inspiration behind the school. His first visit to the town was in 1886, en route to Martinique, but on his return in February 1888 the colony was formed there. Here Gauguin established a style of painting known as *synthétisme*. The Synthetist style was defined by a flat picture plane and bold unnatural colour, with figures drawn in black outline. To the group the ethos of Synthetism meant painting from memory; an impression of a past experience rather than a direct impression from life. The first *synthétismé* exhibition of work was held at the Paris Exposition in 1889 and the *Groupe Synthétiste* was founded two years later in 1891.

PAUL GAUGUIN
(1848–1903)

Pont-Aven School

Gauguin was born in Paris to a French father and Peruvian mother, and from the age of three until seven he lived in Peru, returning to France in 1855. As a young man, in 1870, he became a stockbroker and was painting merely as a hobby. Then after over a decade in finance he chose to paint full-time from 1883. Life as an artist was to be a financially difficult time for him. One of the early exhibitions of his art was with the Impressionist group but by

Paul Gauguin
The Vision after the Sermon (Jacob wrestling with the Angel) **(detail), 1888**
© National Gallery of Scotland, Edinburgh, Scotland/The Bridgeman Art Library

MEDIUM: Oil on canvas

RELATED WORKS: Paul Gauguin, *The Yellow Christ*, 1889

Paul Gauguin
Aha oe Feii? (What, are you Jealous?)
(detail), 1892
© Pushkin Museum, Moscow, Russia/
Giraudon/The Bridgeman Art Library

MEDIUM: Oil on canvas

RELATED WORKS: Paul Gauguin,
The Siesta, 1892–94

the late 1880s, at the age of 40, he was in Pont-Aven creating
works based on the colourful *cloisonné* technique and formulating
his *synthétisme* style. One work from this period stands out above
others. It is *The Vision after the Sermon (Jacob wrestling with the
Angel)*, 1888 (*see* pages 146–47), a fusion of Synthetism, Symbolism
and primitive art. In the painting contemporary Breton peasant
women, wearing distinctive Breton hats, witness the biblical
story of Jacob wrestling with a stranger, who is actually an angel.
Many of the women have their backs to the viewer, although some
are in profile and wonderment is etched on their faces. Gauguin
accentuates the Synthetist use of a two-dimensional picture plane
and strong unreal colour. On Gauguin's return to Paris in 1891 he
shared a residence with the artist Alphonse Mucha (1860–1939),
above a *crémerie*, a café-restaurant with rooms to let, but shortly
afterwards Gauguin was to settle on the island of Tahiti, where he
took a wife. It was here that he painted *Aha oe Feii? (What, are you
Jealous?)*, 1892 (*see* right), depicting two young Tahitian women.
Again the style of painting is primitive, accentuated by a flat
space, and combined with the use of unnatural colours for the
background and the carefully observed figures.

ÉMILE BERNARD (1868–1941)

Emotional Expression

Bernard was born in Lille in 1868 and at the age of 10 he
moved to Paris. By 1888 he had joined Paul Gauguin in Pont-
Aven in Brittany. His major works focus on rural life in France,
particularly in Brittany, and the artworks he created whilst at
Pont-Aven – many created under the guidance of Gauguin
– express emotion through colour and line, eliminating

perspective and emphasizing the artificiality of the flat canvas. He was a founder of the Symbolist art movement, which is one of the roots of Art Nouveau. Bernard wholeheartedly embraced Gauguin's *synthétisme* with its roots in Japanese art, and Bernard came to be noted for his decorative *cloisonné* use

of colour, named after the brightly coloured enamelware, in which each colour is separated from the others by strips of thin metal, a similar effect to that of leaded stained-glass windows. On canvas the style is visible in the dark outlines of the figures and the sections of colour. The intensity of Bernard's use of colour creates a near-abstract work within a representative painting. In *Breton Women with Seaweed*, c. 1892 (*see* left), Bernard uses flat areas of pure colour to depict both the landscape and the women at work.

PAUL SÉRUSIER (1864–1927)

The Talisman

To find a pure expression of Art Nouveau one looks to the French artist Paul Sérusier. Sérusier's father, a successful businessman, gave his son a promising education and in 1875, aged 11, Sérusier had enrolled at the Lycée Condorcet to study Greek and Latin, philosophy and science. However, Sérusier's passion was painting and on leaving school he trained as an artist at the Académie Julian in Paris, where he was a popular and talented painter who would become a mentor at the school. The academy was a desirable alternative to the official École des Beaux-Arts. In the summer of 1888 Sérusier joined other artists of the Pont-Aven School, where he was closely supervised by Gauguin, and that same year Sérusier produced an astonishing artwork in oil on wood panel, titled *Le Talisman (The Talisman)*,

Émile Bernard
Breton Women with Seaweed, c. 1892
Courtesy of Indianapolis Museum of Art, USA/Samuel Josefowitz Collection of the School of Pont-Aven/The Bridgeman Art Library/© ADAGP, Paris and DACS, London 2009

MEDIUM: Oil on canvas

RELATED WORKS: Émile Bernard, *Bridge at Pont-Aven*, 1891

Paul Sérusier
The Talisman (The Swallow-hole in the Bois d'Amour), 1888
© Musée d'Orsay, Paris, France/ Giraudon/The Bridgeman Art Library

MEDIUM: Oil on panel

RELATED WORKS: Paul Sérusier, *Celtic Tale*, 1894

also known as *The Swallow-hole in the Bois d'Amour*, 1888 (*see* page 151). The painting is a synthesis of Abstraction and Symbolism in which the intensity of rich colours creates a tangible image of the artist's experience, where life is observed yet painted as though it were a memory. The essence of its memory evokes emotion, and is painted as an abstract symbol of its being.

Gustav Gurschner
Table lamp, c. 1890
© Estate of Gustav Gurschner/
Private Collection/Photo © Christie's
Images/The Bridgeman Art Library

MEDIUM: Shell and metal

RELATED WORKS: Katsushika Hokusai
(1760–1849), *Kanagarwa-oki nami ura*
(*The Wave*), c. 1830–32

EDVARD MUNCH (1863–1944)

Contribution to Art Nouveau

One associates the Norwegian artist Edvard Munch (1863–1944) with the 'isms' of Symbolism, Expressionism and Synthetism, each a root and branch of *Jugendstil*, the new art appearing in Germany in the late nineteenth century. In 1879 his aim was to study to become an engineer but illness halted his plan and in 1882/83 he took painting lessons at college in Kristiana (now Oslo). Then in 1885 he visited Paris and it was there that Munch was to study the work of other 'isms': Impressionism, Neo-Impressionism and Symbolism, and the 'art nouveau' of the graphic artists who were designing and painting publicity posters and advertisements. Munch's effective visualization of psychological trauma is a branch of the Expressionist movement. His contribution to Art Nouveau, meanwhile, is in synthesis of style, bold colour and graphic interpretation. His use of colour and manipulation of the flat picture plane, too, associate his name with the Art Nouveau movement.

Influence in Germany

Munch returned to Paris to study in the studio of Léon Bonnat (1833–1922). His work began to circulate in French and German art magazines and in 1892 he was invited by the *Verain Berliner Künstler* (Association of Berlin Artists) to exhibit his work at their November exhibition. The controversial content of his paintings was received with criticism, however, and *Gruppe XI* was formed in protest; their support created a bond of friendship between Munch and German artists and writers, including Julius

Edvard Munch
The Scream (The Cry), 1893
Courtesy of Nasjonalgalleriet, Oslo,
Norway/The Bridgeman Art Library/
© Munch Museum/Munch-Ellingsen
Group, BONO, Oslo/DACS, London 2009

MEDIUM: Oil, tempera and pastel
on cardboard

RELATED WORKS: Edvard Munch,
Anxiety, 1894

Meier-Graefe (1867–1935) and Richard Deheml (1863–1920).
Also in Berlin at the time were the Swedish writer, photographer
and painter August Strindberg (1849–1912) and the Norwegian
playwright Henrik Ibsen (1828–1906), for whom Munch
designed stage sets. His friends encouraged Munch to continue
his work, and during his time in Berlin Munch would have been
inspired by many examples of the decorative art of *Jugendstil*, in
the homes and studios of the intellectuals he frequented. Many
such works, in turn, would have been informed by Katushika
Hokusai's (1760–1849), *The Breaking Wave of Kanagawa, c.* 1831.
The *Table lamp, c.* 1890 (*see* left), by the Austrian designer Gustav
Gurschner (1873–1970), in curved silvered metal with a nautilus
shade, is typical of such.

The Scream

The influence of Munch's exposure to many different art forms
in Paris and Berlin can be seen in his painting *The Scream (The
Cry)*, 1893 (*see* right). This work in oil, tempera and pastel on
cardboard is one of several versions. In the picture a fearful
young woman in the foreground stands alone, with her hands
over her ears, drowning out sound and reality. Her oval open
mouth emits a long, silent scream, and the curving shape of her
body mirrors the curving, swirling landscape. She is part of it
and yet set apart by her cry. Other figures in the distance walk
towards her, accentuating her loneliness. Next to her, on the
other side of a wooden balustrade, Munch depicts a swirling
'sea' of landscape and water. Meeting the landscape, the sky
is a fermentation of red, cream and green streaks. By depicting
the woman's state of mind through distorted form and colour,
Munch associates himself with the Symbolists and the emerging
Expressionists. Whilst Munch may introduce perspective in the
distant figures, the vivid unnatural colours he uses highlight the
artificiality of the flat picture plane.

Munch's paintings evoke reality through memory and colour, a Synthetist form of painting. He painted *The Scream* as part of a series entitled *The Frieze of Life*, which focused on aspects of love and death. Munch wrote about this work, 'These paintings are moods, impressions of life of the soul…'. Suffering traumas in his youth, from the manic religious teaching of his father to the death of his parents and siblings, one can understand why he focused on subjects that gave pain, and the melancholy of personal loss is much in evidence in his works, which represent a state of mind rather than a reality.

Munch's Women

Between 1892 and 1908 Munch divided his time between Berlin and Paris and during these years he painted *Madonna*, *c.* 1894–95 (*see* left). In contrast to his painting *Puberty*, 1894, which denotes the innocence and shyness of a naked young girl seated on a bed, facing the viewer, *Madonna* connotes sexuality and a self-awareness of beauty. Both are disconcerting images, however. The half-portrait of the naked young 'Madonna' stands facing the viewer; her nakedness of no consequence to her. Her head is thrown back and bathed in a halo of red. Her long hair, thick and dark, frames her face where it touches her shoulders then reaches down to her waist. One can see here a romantic forerunner

Edvard Munch
Madonna, **1894/5**
Courtesy of Nasjonalgalleriet, Oslo, Norway/The Bridgeman Art Library/© Munch Museum/ Munch-Ellingsen Group, BONO, Oslo/DACS, London 2009

MEDIUM: Oil on canvas

RELATED WORKS: Jean Delville (1867–1953), *Death (La Mort), c.* 1890

of Mucha's decorative semi-naked women and Gustav Klimt's *Judith*, 1901 (*see* page 44). Munch brings the youth of *Puberty* and the eroticism of *Madonna* together in *Woman in Three Stages (Sphinx)*, 1893–95 (*see* below), featuring three full-length depictions of women. Each symbolizes a stage in life from childhood to old age.

Edvard Munch
***Woman in Three Stages
(Sphinx)*, 1893–95**
Courtesy of Rasmus Meyers Samlinger,
Bergen, Norway/The Bridgeman
Art Library/© Munch Museum/

Munch-Ellingsen Group, BONO, Oslo/
DACS, London 2009

MEDIUM: unknown

RELATED WORKS: Edvard Munch,
Puberty, 1894–95

THE NABIS

In Paris in 1888 a rebellious group of disparate but like-minded French artists formed a collective known as *Les Nabis*, the Hebrew word for prophet. Their style was distinctive in its emphasis on the artificiality of the flat surface, a use of bold unnatural colour and line, and inspiration taken from Japanese art.

MAURICE DENIS (1870–1943)

A Leading Light

Maurice Denis (1870–1943), an artist and writer, dabbled in various styles of art and he was to become a leading figure of *Les Nabis*. He stated in an 1890 edition of *La Revue Blanche*, 'Remember, a picture before being a war horse, a nude or an anecdotal subject – is essentially a flat surface covered with colours arranged in a certain order'. In the article 'Definition of Neo-Traditionalism' he went on to define the principles of modern art. His painting *Homage to Cézanne*, 1900, depicts himself and several other members of the Nabis, including Pierre Bonnard (1867–1947), Odilon Redon (1840–1916), Sérusier and Édouard Vuillard (1868–1940), gathering to admire a Cézanne painting. Each took a keen interest in the paintings of Paul Cézanne (1839–1906) and his use of tiny painted 'cubes' of block colour, which built up the picture plane.

Maurice Denis
The Ladder in the Foliage, 1892
Courtesy of Musée Maurice Denis,
St Germain-en-Laye, France/Lauros/
Giraudon/The Bridgeman Art Library/
© ADAGP, Paris and DACS, London 2009

MEDIUM: Oil on canvas

RELATED WORKS: François Boucher
(1703–70), *The Rape of Europa,* 1747

**Louis Majorelle and
Auguste Daum**
Magnolia lamps, 1903
© Private Collection/Photo © Christie's
Images/The Bridgeman Art Library

MEDIUM: Bronze and glass

RELATED WORKS: Hector Guimard,
Palais Royale Métro Entrance, Paris, c. 1900

Rococo Style

Denis's work *The Ladder in the Foliage*, 1892 (*see* left), also known as *Poetic Arabesques for the Decoration of a Ceiling* is a decorative ceiling panel in oil on canvas. The painting belongs to a key period in his career when Denis adopted a Synthetist style. The imagery and layout show the influences of Japanese prints, the Rococo revival and the Nabis interest in decorative art. In the painting the four young women, in various stages of ascendancy, are wearing long, romantically swirling dresses and they climb a ladder towards a dark sky, which is broken by patches of light. The movement of their clothing creates an arabesque, serpentine shape; their clothing and the ladder are all depicted in the same colour tones, highlighting the artificiality of the painted flat surface.

Applied Art and Fine Art

In 1923 a former member of the Nabis, Jan Verkade (1868–1946), wrote about its history, and focusing on the group's amalgamation of applied art and fine art, he recalled the Nabis code, which was reiterated by every member of the group: 'No more easel paintings! Down with these useless objects ... there are no

paintings, there are only decorations'. Denis's ceiling painting is an excellent example of their unique approach and his decorative style mirrored the craft pieces in production. The *Magnolia lamps*, 1903 (*see* page 157), in gilt bronze and carved glass, created by Louis Majorelle (1859–1926) and Auguste Daum (1853–1909), are fine examples of this cross-pollination between art and design.

PIERRE BONNARD
(1867–1947)

Pure Colour

Pierre Bonnard worked as a painter, lithographer, book illustrator and designer. In 1888 he attended the École des Beaux-Arts in Paris and the Académie Julian in 1889 and it was here that he met Sérusier, Bernard, Vuillard and Félix Édouard Vallotton (1865–1925), who together would form part of the Nabis group. They exhibited collectively for the first time at the Café Volpini, in Paris, in 1889. Bonnard was one of the first in the group, apart from Gauguin, to use pure colour in his paintings. From the 1890s his artworks accentuate two-dimensional artificiality, particularly in the style of the Japanese decorative silhouette, which formed the basis of the Art Nouveau style.

Fashionable Interiors

A craze for decorative panels (*panneaux décoratifs*) had crossed all fields of art and Alphonse Mucha was producing series upon series of graphic-art panels to decorate the walls of bourgeois apartments. Designers were creating silk and painted folding screens for their clients and the Nabis group, following Gauguin's lead, developed a new language for the art, which focused on painting as decoration. Denis, Bonnard, Vuillard and Ker Xavier Roussel (1867–1944) each created decorative room

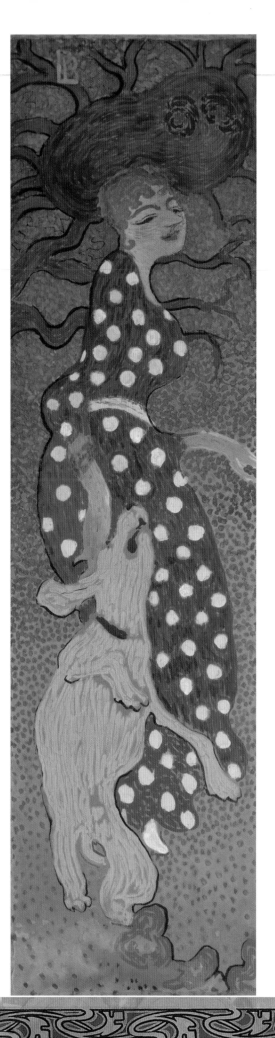

panels for the domestic interior, ranging from ceiling panels to
wall murals and screens. It was a total design experience, where
paintings, panels and screens complemented the room setting.

Women in the Garden

In 1890 and 1891, Bonnard created a series of four panels titled
Women in the Garden. He planned to exhibit them as one screen at
the 1891 *Salon des Indépendents* in Paris, but just before it opened
Bonnard changed his mind as he considered they would be more
decorative as individual paintings. So he took the four-panelled
screen apart and exhibited each separately, in a series of paintings:
Decorative Panel: 1, 2, 3, 4. Each of the panels is narrow and oblong
in shape, which had allowed Bonnard to paint each woman in full
length. One panel, *Woman in a Checked Dress* (*see* far left), depicts
from the rear a young woman in stylish checked dress and large
hat, as she walks through the lush green gardens. In contrast,
Woman in a White Spotted Dress (*see* left) depicts a young woman
turning her head towards the viewer while playing with her dog,
which jumps up towards her. She wears a red dress with white
polka dots and her hairs fly upward. Its flat depiction accentuates
the artificiality of the artwork and its function as pure decoration.

PAUL-ELIE RANSON
(1863–1909)

Firm Friendships

Paul-Elie Ranson (1863–1909) was born in Limoges. He entered the École des Arts Décoratifs in 1886 and then moved to the Académie Julian where he met Bonnard, Sérusier and Denis, forming firm friendships with each of them. Ranson's studio became a meeting place for the friends who, alongside Vuillard and Roussel, formed the Nabis. Ranson's interests were wide in range and he engaged the group in debates on theosophy, which mirrored the Symbolist rejection of natural form. Ranson was noted, too, for his large collection of literature on mysticism and the occult, a fact that drew the critics' attention to his artworks, to look for evidence of such themes within the decorative detail.

Stained Glass

Ranson was possibly instrumental in introducing the art of decorative-panel painting to the group. In 1895 his skill in applied art brought him to the attention of Siegfried Bing (1838–1905), who placed one of Ranson's stained-glass works within the interior of a room setting by van de Velde, at La Maison de l'Art Nouveau, in 1895. His ability as a designer of decorative art, particularly panel paintings and tapestries, book illustrations and ceramics, earned Ranson his place in the Nabis.

Magical Paintings

Ranson's 1892 painting *Women in the Wood* (*see* left) has the decorative quality of a woodcut. In the picture, two women are shown, each wearing a long and loose green dress with a different pattern. They each have long blonde wavy hair, and one stands with her back to the viewer, while the other sits on the ground looking at her reflection in a small pool of water.

Paul-Elie Ranson
Women in the Wood, 1892
© Galerie L'Ergastere, Paris, France/
The Bridgeman Art Library

MEDIUM: Oil on canvas

RELATED WORKS: Carel Nicolaas Storm
van Gravesande (1841–1924), *Forest Path
(Entrée de Forêt),* c. 1885

Paul-Elie Ranson
Foxgloves, 1899
© Galerie L'Ergastere, Paris, France/
The Bridgeman Art Library

MEDIUM: Oil on canvas

RELATED WORKS: Paul-Elie Ranson,
Nabi Landscape, c. 1890

In the background three trees, bare of leaves, are painted with branches raised like arms in the wind. The artist used a black line to accentuate the curvaceous figures of the women, which mirror the curving trunks of the trees. There is an element of

fertile sexuality in the mirror images of the trees and the women, relating to the theosophical view that all that is in the world is from one source. *Foxgloves,* 1899 (*see* left and right), is another seductive image, with its symbol of fertility. The colourful spires of the foxglove (*digitalis*), alongside many other plant species, curve sensuously towards a young woman who stands deep in thought, holding the stem of a flower in her hands. The sinuous curves plant tendrils, in Art Nouveau 'whiplash' lines, mirror the curves of the woman's body, seen in profile.

ÉDOUARD VUILLARD
(1868-1940)

The Intellectual

Édouard Vuillard was a painter, draughtsman and printmaker. Denis wrote of him, 'The outstanding quality of his painting is intelligence', and the remark mirrors the intellect of a man who questioned everything. In a group of creative people, as the Nabis undoubtedly were, they looked to him as the intellectual. Vuillard was born in Paris to a modest-income family and helped his mother and sister in their dressmaking business and this practical introduction to fashion may account for his attention to fabrics and interiors in his art. An education at Lycée Condorcet was to add to his experiences, introducing him to writers and musicians and the artist Denis, and it was through his friendship with Roussel that he took up painting. He attended Académie Julian in 1886 and passed exams for the École des Beaux-Arts in 1887.

Attention to Detail

Vuillard's paintings are recognized for their extraordinary technical expertise and he was described as an 'intimist' painter;

for him an interior-room setting was a complexity of colour and pattern. An outdoor scene, *The Public Gardens: Young Girls Playing and the Interrogation*, 1894 (*see* below left), meanwhile, depicts a landscape of mothers, nannies and children in the park. Vuillard combined the scenery of two Parisian parks: the Tuileries Gardens and the Bois de Boulogne. The painting was part of a commission from the wealthy Alexandre Natanson (1867–1936) and was one of nine painted panels depicting scenes in the public gardens of Paris, destined for the dining room of Natanson's house on the Avenue du Bois. In this panel, a young woman bends down to speak to her young daughter. It is possibly a portrayal of Natanson's wife Olga and their daughter.

Portraits of Memory

Vuillard was a good portrait painter who received many commissions. In each portrayal he merged his role as portraitist with that of a painter of interiors. He enjoyed painting portraits of his family and close friends. *Vallotton and Misia in the Dining Room at rue Saint-Florentin*, 1899 (*see* right), is painted in oil on cardboard and the two people portrayed are the painter Vallotton and Misia Natanson (1872–1950), Vuillard's patron. Both are enveloped in a sea of colours, shape and pattern that are given as much attention as the people present. Vuillard accurately depicts the room setting in some ways, but his use of colour highlights the artificiality of the flattened pattern.

Édouard Vuillard
The Public Gardens: Young Girls Playing and the Interrogation, **1894**
Courtesy of Musée d'Orsay, Paris, France/Giraudon/The Bridgeman Art Library/© ADAGP, Paris and DACS, London 2009

MEDIUM: Distemper on canvas

RELATED WORKS: Andō Hiroshige (1797–1858), *Seba*, late 1830s

Édouard Vuillard
Vallotton and Misia in the Dining Room at rue Saint-Florentin, **1899**
Courtesy of Private Collection/Flammarion/The Bridgeman Art Library/© ADAGP, Paris and DACS, London 2009

MEDIUM: Oil on cardboard

RELATED WORKS: Pierre Bonnard, *The Dressing Room*, 1892

164

KER XAVIER ROUSSEL

(1867–1944)

Symbolism and Decadence

Roussel was born François Xavier Roussel
(1867–1944) in Lorry-lès-Metz, Moselle. He studied
at the Lycée Condorcet in Paris from the age of 15
and it was there that he met Vuillard and they became
lifelong friends. He married Vuillard's sister Marie in
1893 and it was Roussel who persuaded Vuillard to
take up painting instead of an army career. Roussel
favoured painting outdoor scenes and his favourite
subject involved pagan or mythological imagery, and
his use of colour produced a mystical quality in his
works. The lack of spatial depth added a Japanese
quality to his art and his style was very much in the
spirit of Art Nouveau, combining, too, the trends
of Symbolism and decadence depicted in rich colour.
The Terrace at the Tuileries, c. 1892–93 (*see* right),
depicts a casual scene in a park, with people lazing
on the grass and it is a typical scene from the Tuileries,
but Roussel's use of unnatural colour creates a sense
that it is a memory or symbolic moment in the park,
rather than reality. The panel is one of a series of
three, including *The Reunion of Women*, c. 1892–93
and *Conversation in a Garden*, c. 1892–93.

Ker Xavier Roussel
The Terrace at the Tuileries,
c. 1892–93
Courtesy of Musée d'Orsay, Paris,
France/Giraudon/The Bridgeman Art
Library/© ADAGP, Paris and DACS,
London 2009

MEDIUM: Oil on canvas

RELATED WORKS: Georges
Seurat (1859–91), *The Beach at
Gravelines, c.* 1890

FÉLIX ÉDOUARD VALLOTTON
(1865–1925)

Strong, Pure Colour

Vallotton was born in Lausanne, Switzerland. His family were comfortable and middle class and Vallotton received a good education, graduating with a degree in classical studies. In 1882, directly after graduating, he became a naturalized Frenchman and moved to Paris and in 1900 and it was here that Vallotton studied art at the Académie Julian. Prior to the formation of the Nabis, his circle of friends included Charles Cottet (1863–1935) and Henri de Toulouse-Lautrec (1864–1901). Vallotton was a remarkable engraver in wood, reviving interest in the skill of the craft; he was also a painter, printmaker and writer and his graphic art is considered to have influenced Aubrey Beardsley (1872–98) and Munch. It was Cottet, a good friend of Vallotton, who introduced him to the Nabis group, which he joined in 1892. Initially Vallotton preferred to paint landscapes, portraits and portrayals of women. However, his style developed to include interiors and scenes of city life, for example in *The Luxembourg Gardens*, 1895 (*see* left). The paintings of Vallotton were created in the style of a reductive woodcut. His use of strong, pure colour, with emphasis on outline and flat patterns aligned his works to Symbolism and Art Nouveau, for example in *Moonlight*, 1894.

Félix Édouard Vallotton
The Luxembourg Gardens
(detail), 1895
© Private Collection/The Bridgeman
Art Library

MEDIUM: Oil on canvas

RELATED WORKS: Édouard Vuillard,
*The Public Gardens: Young Girls Playing and
the Interrogation*, 1894

Odilon Redon
Ophelia among the Flowers,
c. 1905–08
© National Gallery, London, UK/
The Bridgeman Art Library

MEDIUM: Pastel on paper

RELATED WORKS: John Everett
Millais (1829–96), *Ophelia,* 1852

René Lalique
Pendant brooch and chain,
c. 1899–1902
Courtesy of Christie's Images Ltd/
© ADAGP, Paris and DACS, London 2009

MEDIUM: Enamel, ivory, gold and pearl

RELATED WORKS: Louis Comfort
Tiffany, *Blown Favrile glass vase, c.* 1900

ODILON REDON
(1840–1916)

Early Inspiration

Bertrand-Jean Redon was born in
Bordeaux and received the nickname
Odilon from his mother who was
called Odile. His talent as an artist
was recognized at the age of 10 and
he began training from the age of 15.
His father had wanted him to study as
an architect, but Redon failed to gain
entry to the École des Beaux-Arts,
so entailing a change of plan, though
he was later to enter it to study art,
where he was mentored by Jean-Léon
Gérôme (1824–1904). The formality
of the classical academic teaching of
art by Gérôme did not suit Redon or
his own particular style of painting,
and he left his studies and joined the
army. Redon fought in the Franco-
Prussian war of 1870, then on his
return to civilian life he lived in Paris
where he worked as a lithographer
and engraver, and his paintings in
pastel and oil were influenced by

the Realist painter Gustave Courbet (1819–77) amongst others,
although soon after the death of Courbet, Redon turned to
charcoal as his medium. Redon published an album of works
titled *Dans le Rêve* in 1879 and recognition of this work was given
a publicity boost when Joris-Karl Huysmans (1848–1907), the
author of a strangely mystifying novel, *À Rebours (Against Nature),*
1884, included reference to Redon's work in his book. Huysmans'
'decadent' book was associated with the Symbolist movement.

Colour and Symbolism

Involvement with the Nabis for Redon came at the end of the
century, when he exhibited with them. The *fin-de-siècle* decadent
style and use of unnatural colour links Redon firmly to the Art
Nouveau movement, seen for
instance in *Ophelia among the Flowers,*
c. 1905–08 (*see* far left), which
refers to the death of Ophelia in the
play *Hamlet,* 1599–1601, by William
Shakespeare (1564–1616). In the
play Ophelia, the tragic heroine,
drowns when a willow branch
breaks and she falls into the river.
Redon depicts her in a mystical
landscape; the unidentifiable
flowers are splashed on leaves
in unnatural shades of green
and a vibrant, unworldly blue.
The pastel work illustrates
Redon's ability to create,
through colour, an image of
a timeless place, beyond death.
This work is contemporary to the
jewellery design of René Lalique
(1860–1945) for a *Pendant brooch
and chain, c.* 1899–1902 (*see* left).
Here Lalique employed the same
colour tones as Redon was to
choose: a combination of soft pinks,
blues, creams and gold, created
in enamel, ivory, gold and pearl.

LES VINGT

Belgian art in the 1880s and 1890s was a mix of European styles, leading towards Art Nouveau. *Les Vingt*, a group formed in Brussels of like-minded artists – not all Belgian – drew the most innovative artists to their city and their paintings were informed by artists such as Gauguin, Georges Seurat (1859–91) and Vincent van Gogh (1853–90). The artists of *Les Vingt* found a new audience and Brussels vied with Paris as the capital of Art Nouveau. Belgian decorative design, particularly works by Henry van de Velde (1863–1957), became sought-after pieces, drawing global attention from the arts market.

HENRY VAN DE VELDE
(1863-1957)

Vibrant Contrasts

The diverse talents of van de Velde are evident in his work as an artist, industrial and decorative-arts designer, and in his work as an art critic. His name is linked to stylistic change in architecture and decorative art in Belgium in the 1880s, and he also made a substantial contribution to Art Nouveau through his paintings. Van de Velde studied painting at the Académie des Beaux-Arts in Antwerp from 1881 to 1884 and, crucially, for a further year in Paris under the French Academic painter, Charles-Auguste-Émile Durand (a.k.a. Carolus-Duran) (1837–1917). This exposed him

Henry van de Velde
The Haymaker, c. 1891–92
© Estate of Henry van de Velde/Petit Palais, Geneva, Switzerland/Peter Willi/ The Bridgeman Art Library

MEDIUM: Oil on canvas

RELATED WORKS: Pierre Bonnard, *The Croquet Party*, 1891–92

Henry van de Velde
La Veillée des Anges textile hanging, 1893
© Estate of Henry van deVelde/ Kunstgewerbe Museum, Zurich, Switzerland/ The Bridgeman Art Library

MEDIUM: Textile

RELATED WORKS: Itō Jakuchû (1716–1800), *Chrysanthemums by a Stream with Rocks*, 1760

to vibrant contrasts in painting styles. Between the years 1886 to 1887 one can see Belgian artists, including van de Velde, taking note of the *pointilliste* technique of the French artist Seurat, which was based on the latest scientific discoveries in the field of optics. From 1888 van de Velde began to paint in this Neo-Impressionist style and evidence of this can be seen in his *Portrait of Laurent van de Velde*, 1888.

Translations in Colour

The quality of van de Velde's paintings resulted in his election to *Les Vingt* (also known as *Les Bubonnistes*, a nickname given to them by local art critics as a 'bubonic plague' on traditional art) in November 1888 and he exhibited artworks at the annual Salon of *Les Vingt* in 1889. Six paintings sent by the Dutch artist van Gogh for inclusion in the 1890 exhibition led to a further change in van de Velde's artistic development. Van Gogh had included *Red Vineyards near Arles (Mont-Majour)*, 1888 and *Wheat Field, Sunrise*, 1889 among the six. Van de Velde translated the intensely colourful works to inform paintings such as *The Haymaker*, *c.* 1891–92 (*see* left), and in this work van de Velde turned his interest towards a literary interpretation of Symbolism, to represent a deeper reality. He was guided by friends Paul Verlaine (1844–96) and Stéphane (Étienne) Mallarmé (1842–98), both French authors and Symbolist poets. Van de Velde explored a symbolic depiction of haymakers in his use of vibrant contrast highlighting the two-dimensional picture space. A textile wall hanging, *La Veillée des Anges*, 1893 (*see* above), also reflects this technique.

GEORGES LEMMEN
(1865–1916)

Early Influences

Georges Lemmen was born in Schaerbeek, near Brussels. His father was an architect and Lemmen took lessons in drawing at a school in Sint Joost-ten-Noode, possibly with the aim of following his father's career. However, he gave up drawing, perhaps not ready to commit to the discipline. On graduating from school he turned to painting and exhibited some of his works in galleries over the next three years. His work was of a high standard and he joined *Les Vingt* in 1888, at the age of 23, and there he met Théo van Rysselberghe (1862–1926), who introduced Lemmen to the work of the French Neo-Impressionist, Seurat. The style of Lemmen's work, particularly in *The Beach at Heist*, 1891–92 (*see* below), is decidedly inspired by Seurat, both in its Pointillist execution and use of rolling colour throughout the picture plane. Like Seurat, Lemmen has produced a carefully calculated composition, using vibrant primary colours to execute the work.

Lemmen changed his style again in 1895, turning away from Pointillism to embrace Art Nouveau in many forms, from paintings to book illustrations, to posters, pastels and ceramics.

THÉO VAN RYSSELBERGHE (1862–1926)

Pointillist Style

The Flemish artist van Rysselberghe was born in Ghent and he attended the local Académie des Beaux-Arts, followed by a move to the Académie in Brussels. At the age of 18 he successfully exhibited two works in the Brussels Salon. Two years later, in November 1883, he became a founding member of *Les Vingt*. Following his visit to France to see the work of Seurat in 1886, a major exhibition of Neo-Impressionist works was organized by *Les Vingt* in 1887 and that same year Rysselberghe had changed his style of painting to Neo-Impressionism, following the Pointillist method of painting with pure dots or dashes of colour, as practised by Seurat, Paul Signac (1863–1935) and others. Rysselberghe used a *tachisme* method of short brush strokes of pure colour, choosing complementary luminescent colours to bring the painting to life. *The Straw Hat*, 1890 (*see* right), is a good example of this technique. The following year he encouraged a new member of *Les Vingt*, Lemmen, to change to the Pointillist style but 10 years later, in 1898, Rysselberghe himself had tired of this method.

Georges Lemmen
The Beach at Heist, 1891–92
© Musée d'Orsay, Paris, France/
The Bridgeman Art Library

MEDIUM: Oil on canvas

RELATED WORKS: Georges Seurat
(1859–91), *Porte-en-Bessin, High Tide*, 1888–89

Théo van Rysselberghe
The Straw Hat, 1890
© Private Collection/© Whitford & Hughes,
London, UK/The Bridgeman Art Library

MEDIUM: Oil on canvas

RELATED WORKS: Georges Seurat
(1859–91), *The Gardener*, 1882–83

Jan Toorop
Song of the Times, 1893
© Haags Gemeentemuseum, The Hague,
Netherlands/The Bridgeman Art Library

MEDIUM: Chalk on wood

RELATED WORKS: Puvis de Chavannes
(1824–98), *Hope*, 1872

JAN TOOROP
(1858–1928)

Symbolist Preoccupations

Jan Toorop (1858–1928) moved from his birthplace in Java
when he was 14, and began his official artistic training in Delft
and Amsterdam between 1876 and 1882, before finally settling
in Brussels where he completed his education in 1885 and became
a founder member of *Les Vingt*. His early paintings were in the
main Impressionist in style, but he began to emulate James Ensor
(1860–1949), a fellow founder of *Les Vingt*, in his application of thick
paint using a palette knife. By the end of the decade his paintings
had become darker in mood, reflecting Symbolist preoccupations
concerning the human condition, the rejection of materialism and
the polarities of good and evil. Both elements exist in *Song of the
Times* (or *Song of the Ages*), 1893 (*see* left), often overlapping each
other, just as in human nature. It has been suggested that the figures
with the long flowing hair are borrowed from Toorop's own
Javanese culture, but they are also redolent of other sources that
make up the eclectic mix of Art Nouveau influences. His use of
wood as a ground would, however, suggest that the artist was also
being true to his own Indonesian culture, which reveres the use of
the material in sculpture. The development of the curvilinear style
by Margaret MacDonald Mackintosh (1865–1933) was in tandem
with Toorop rather than either influencing the other. Margaret was
not an artist associated with Symbolism, but her work in Glasgow
is said to have belonged to the 'spook school' of art, that shared a
similar interest in the macabre. This is evident in her *Panel of beaten
metal*, 1898–99 (*see* page 177), part of a fire screen made to show
at the Vienna *Secession* exhibition of 1900.

Jan Toorop
The Three Fiancées, 1893
© Rijksmuseum Kroller-Muller, Otterlo,
Netherlands/The Bridgeman Art Library

MEDIUM: unknown

RELATED WORKS: Fernand Hodler
(1853–1918), *Day I, 1899–1900*

**Margaret MacDonald
Mackintosh**
Panel of beaten metal, 1898–99
© Glasgow University Art Gallery,
Scotland/The Bridgeman Art Library

MEDIUM: Beaten metal

RELATED WORKS: Gustav Klimt,
Hostile Forces (from the Beethoven frieze), 1902

He particularly encouraged the use of geometric forms, akin to mosaic patterning in their execution and it is this that seems to have had a profound effect also on Gustav Klimt (1862–1918), who drew on the same inspiration. Apart from painting, Toorop was also interested in the decorative arts and was commissioned several times by the Catholic Church to execute stained-glass work. For these and his subsequent paintings he developed a style of portraiture that was considered avant-garde, the faces often having angular features emphasized by the strong use of colour. Toorop never lost the sense of mysticism and Symbolism in his work, despite their modern aesthetic.

Javanese Arts

In Toorop's *The Three Fiancées*, 1893 (*see* left), the figures with their long tendril-like arms are redolent of the Javanese puppet theatres (*Wayang Kulit*) of his homeland culture. This performing art form is at least 2,000 years old, but later, under Islamic law, which forbids the portrayal of gods in human form, the Javanese adapted the performance to show the depiction of the shadow of the figures instead. The artist explained his work of *The Three Fiancées* as follows, 'the central fiancée evokes an inward, superior desire … and an ideal suffering…. The fiancée on the left symbolizes spiritual suffering. She is the mystic fiancée her eyes wide with fear…'. And he stated that the third figure had 'a materialistic and profane expression'.

Toorop the Socialist

In common with many artists of this period, Toorop was drawn towards politics and the problems of oppression and the underclasses in society. Where his French counterparts would read Mallarmé, Toorop read Maurice Maeterlinck (1862–1949), the Belgian Nobel prize-winning author. Unlike Maeterlinck, however, who rejected his Catholic past, Toorop embraced the religion, having himself and his daughter Charley baptized in 1905. Shortly after this, Toorop began painting religious scenes based very much on the theories of Father Desiderius Lenz (1832–1928), a monk who was the first principal of the Beuron Art School and who advocated a return to large-scale religious mural painting, using early Renaissance and Byzantine styling.

JOHAN THORN PRIKKER
(1868–1932)

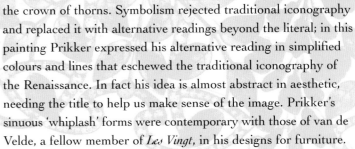

Sinuous Forms

Another Symbolist painter was the
Dutch artist Johan Thorn Prikker
(1868–1932), also influenced by the
teachings of the Beuron Art School.
The Bride of Christ, 1892 (*see* left and
right), depicts a young woman wearing
a white dress and a tiara resembling
the crown of thorns. Symbolism rejected traditional iconography
and replaced it with alternative readings beyond the literal; in this
painting Prikker expressed his alternative reading in simplified
colours and lines that eschewed the traditional iconography of
the Renaissance. In fact his idea is almost abstract in aesthetic,
needing the title to help us make sense of the image. Prikker's
sinuous 'whiplash' forms were contemporary with those of van de
Velde, a fellow member of *Les Vingt*, in his designs for furniture.

After 1896 Prikker moved away from painting and
concentrated instead on the decorative arts, executing designs
for stained glass and mosaics. He also became a teacher of
applied arts at Krefeld in Germany and showed his work at
the Vienna *Secession* exhibitions. In 1920 he became head of
the stained-glass department at the *Kunstgewerbeschule* (Academy
School) in Munich, and later worked in the *Deutscher Werkbund*.
He enjoyed considerable success disseminating his progressive
ideas in design.

Johan Thorn Prikker
The Bride of Christ, 1892
© Rijksmuseum Kroller-Muller, Otterlo,
Netherlands/The Bridgeman Art Library

MEDIUM: unknown

RELATED WORKS: Aubrey Beardsley,
John and Salomé, 1894

Gustav Klimt
Portrait of Hermine Gallia, 1904
© National Gallery, London, UK/
The Bridgeman Art Library

MEDIUM: Oil on canvas

RELATED WORKS: John Singer Sargent
(1856–1925), *Portrait of Lady Agnew*, 1892

THE VIENNA SECESSION

The Viennese *Secession* was formed in 1897 of 19 artists and designers including Koloman Moser (1868–1918), Josef Hoffmann (1870–1956) and Klimt, all of whom rejected the conservative attitude towards the arts of the *Künstlerhaus* (Academy) in favour of a more modern experimental approach, seeing themselves as a regenerative force. They launched a magazine named *Ver Sacrum* ('sacred spring') to promulgate their new artistic forms of expression appropriate for the dawning of the new century.

GUSTAV KLIMT (1862–1918)

Avant-garde Influences

Klimt was born just outside Vienna, the eldest of seven children. His father was an engraver and encouraged his son to enter the *Kunstgewerbeschule* at the age of 14. His early work is in an academic style and won him a gold medal presented by Emperor Franz Josef (1830–1916) for one of his many mural paintings in the city. His most important work in that style was for Vienna University in 1894, but by this time his interest in traditional painting was waning as he began to be influenced by the avant-garde Symbolist painters such as Toorop. Klimt formally seceded from the academy in 1897 becoming the *Secession*'s first president at a time when Art Nouveau was coming into its own. His own interpretation of the style led him to become one of the world's greatest decorative artists.

Gustav Klimt *(overleaf)*
Here's a Kiss to the Whole World!,
detail from *the Beethoven Frieze*, 1902
© Osterreichische Galerie Belvedere,
Vienna, Austria/The Bridgeman Art Library

MEDIUM: Mixed media on stucco

RELATED WORKS: Max Klinger
(1857–1920), *Sculpture of Beethoven for
the Secession Building*, 1902

The Total Work of Art

In 1899 Klimt and the rest of the Secessionists, bolstered by the success of their first exhibition, embarked upon building a permanent exhibition hall, designed by Joseph Maria Olbrich (1867–1908). As part of the decorative scheme for the interior, Klimt worked on *The Beethoven Frieze*, 1902 (*see* pages 180–81). The entire frieze exemplified the work of the Secessionist group of artists, aspiring to create the *Gesamtkunstwerk* or 'total work of art'. It celebrated both the composer and the fourteenth exhibition of the Secessionist group. The scheme involved a sculpture of Beethoven by Max Klinger (1857–1920) (a *Gesamtkunstwerk* in its own right) and a series of decorative wall panels by Klimt, inspired by Beethoven's 'Ninth Symphony' and depicting aspects of the human condition. The panel seen on pages 180–81 is part of the 'arts' wall and depicts a female choir singing the final part of the symphony 'Ode to Joy'. The painted panels were highly decorated with gold leaf and semi-precious stones.

The Haute Bourgeois

Klimt's *Portrait of Hermine Gallia*, 1904 (*see* page 179), is typical of his Secessionist work, a portrait of an haute bourgeois woman. In 1893, Hermine (1870–1936) had married her uncle Moritz Gallia (active 1890s), an enthusiastic patron of the arts, and by the time this painting was commissioned Klimt had made a name for himself as a portrait artist of exceptionally innovative talents. Many of his clients were wives of the prominent Jewish bourgeoisie including the banker Fritz Wärndorfer (1868–1939) who later financed and

Gustav Klimt
Minerva or *Pallas Athena*,
(detail), *c.* 1898
© Wien Museum Karlsplatz, Vienna,
Austria/The Bridgeman Art Library

MEDIUM: unknown

RELATED WORKS: Gustav Klimt,
Cover of *Ver Sacrum*, 1898

Gustav Klimt
Fritza von Riedler (detail), 1906
© Österreichische Galerie Belvedere,
Vienna, Austria/The Bridgeman Art Library

MEDIUM: Oil on canvas

RELATED WORKS: Gustav Klimt,
Portrait of Hermine Gallia, 1904

patronized the *Wiener Werkstätte*. Unlike any portrait painter before or since, Klimt's paintings are usually encrusted with semi-precious stones and use copious amounts of gold leaf, reflecting the status of his clients. For Klimt they, too, are an example of a *Gesamtkunstwerk* that combines the fine and decorative arts.

Collaboration with Hoffmann

Another example of the perfect *Gesamtkunstwerk* was the *Palais Stoclet* (*see* below), in Brussels, built by fellow Secessionist Josef Hoffmann between 1905 and 1911 for the industrialist Adolphe Stoclet (1871–1949). The house was the apogee of the Art Nouveau style, the ultimate masterpiece of interior design, although built at a time when the style was on the wane. The simplified forms and geometric shape of the building anticipate the post-war Modernism of the 1920s, except that the exterior was clad in marble. To match the lavish use of this material Klimt

was commissioned to help create the interiors, and the result was a real *tour de force* of design. Like any good patron, Stoclet allowed Hoffmann and Klimt a free hand in the design of the house and interior, with an unlimited budget. The dining room was a particularly wonderful example of a *Gesamtkunstwerk* between Hoffmann and Klimt. Hoffmann used marble cladding for the walls and designed the furniture; Klimt meanwhile created a number of mosaic panels. The resulting frieze in mosaic form using gold and semi-precious stones was similar to the *Beethoven* work, but was on an altogether grander scale reflecting the status of his client. Klimt had learned the skills at the Vienna School of Arts and Crafts 30 years before, but after seeing the mosaics in Ravenna in 1903 he reinvented the technique to accommodate modern-abstract designs. Stoclet was a collector of oriental art and it is clear from the designs that Klimt executed that he wished to recreate some of those influences in the mosaics. There is also a sense of the Byzantine influences in this work. The *Tree of Life*, *c.* 1905–09 (*see* above and right), is the central theme of the frieze.

The Romantic Embrace

One of the panels in the Stoclet frieze is of a couple embracing and is based on Klimt's earlier painting, *The Kiss*, 1907–08 (*see* page 186), probably the artist's most-famous work. This earlier work is of the artist himself in an embrace with his companion and probable lover

Josef Hoffmann
Palais Stoclet, 1905–11
© Estate of Josef Hoffmann/
The Bridgeman Art Library

MEDIUM: Architecture

RELATED WORKS: Joseph Maria
Olbrich, *Secession Building in Vienna*, 1898–99

Gustav Klimt
Tree of Life, from *the Stoclet
Frieze*, *c.* 1905–09
© MAK (Austrian Museum of Applied Arts),
Vienna, Austria/The Bridgeman Art Library

MEDIUM: unknown

RELATED WORKS: Antoni Gaudí,
Mosaics for the Parc Güell, Barcelona, c. 1900

Emilie Flöge (1874–1952). The work is the culmination of Klimt's so-called 'Golden period' in which he used excessive quantities of gold-leaf inlays, semi-precious stones and enamels to create his own *Gesamtkunstwerk*. The background consists of gold swirls, but the extravaganza is reserved for the couple's costumes. Unlike his previous portraits that show self-assured and even assertive women, this one reveals her as submissive, a reflection perhaps of the artist's own self-assurance as an unmarried lover who is said to have fathered at least 14 children. However, the portrait has been the subject of much subsequent debate as to whether there is a tension between the couple suggesting in fact that Klimt and Flöge were not lovers at all. Either way, the work is based very much on examples of Byzantine and Japanese motifs in Klimt's own collection of paintings and artefacts.

Attraction to Emilie

Flöge was a well-respected couturier in Vienna between 1904 and the Nazi-German *Anschluss* of 1938, forming the *Schwest Flöge* with her sisters Helene and Pauline. Klimt was attracted to the reform of clothing in the same way as he had seen the necessity for it in the arts, that is, for it to be more innovative and creative in its aesthetic. What attracted him to this particular couturier was Emilie's use of the folk motif. There are various photographs in existence that show both Klimt and Flöge wearing loose-fitting garments, some of which were designed by the artist. One gets a sense of the creative aspects of these garments most fully in *The Kiss*, 1907–08. However, in his portrait of her, *Emilie Flöge*, 1902 (*see* right), she is wearing a close-fitting gown that shows her waspish shape to reveal a very sensuous woman. The gown has an exaggerated collar and ruff redolent of the Elizabethan age that sought to highlight the woman's face, personifying her as an earthly deity.

Gustav Klimt
The Kiss, 1907–08
© Osterreichische Galerie Belvedere,
Vienna, Austria/The Bridgeman Art Library

MEDIUM: Oil on canvas

RELATED WORKS: Auguste Rodin
(1840–1917), *The Kiss*, 1889

Gustav Klimt
Emilie Flöge (detail), 1902
© Wien Museum Karlsplatz, Vienna,
Austria/The Bridgeman Art Library

MEDIUM: Oil on canvas

RELATED WORKS: Marcus Gheeraerts
the Younger (1561–1636), *Portrait of
Elizabeth I (The Dychley Portrait)*, 1592

FURTHER READING

Arwas, V., *Berthon and Grasset*, Academy Editions, Paris, 1978

Chassé, C., *The Nabis and the Period*, Lund Humphries, London, 1969 (translated by Michael Bullock)

Collins, M., *Towards Post-Modernism*, British Museum, London, 1994

Denvir, B., *Toulouse-Lautrec*, Thames & Hudson, London, 1991

Ducray, M., *Vallotton: Gallery of the Arts*, 5 Continents Editions, Milan, 2007

Duncan, A., *Art Nouveau*, Thames & Hudson, London, 1994

Eckert Boyer, P., *The Nabis and the Parisian Avant-Garde*, Rutgers University Press, New Brunswick and London, 1988 (exhibition catalogue)

Escritt, S., *Art Nouveau*, Phaidon Press Ltd, London, 2000

Gibson, M., *Symbolism*, Taschen, Bonn, 1995

Greenhalgh, E. (Ed.), *Art Nouveau: 1890–1914*, V&A Publications, London, 2000

Groom, G., *Beyond the Easel: Decorative Painting by Bonnard, Vuillard, Denis and Roussel, 1890–1930*, The Art Institute of Chicago and Yale University Press, London and New Haven, 2001 (exhibition catalogue)

Hillier, B., *Posters*, Spring Books, London, 1974

Howard, J., *Art Nouveau International*, Manchester University Press, Manchester, 1996

Hutchison, H., *The Poster: An Illustrated History from 1860–1900*, Studio Vista, London, 1968

Johnson, D.C., *American Art Nouveau*, Harry N. Abrams, New York, 1979

Koch, R., *Will H. Bradley: An American Artist in Print*, Hudson Hills Press LLC, Manchester, Vermont, 2002

Madsen, S.T., *Sources of Art Nouveau*, H. Aschehoug & Co. (W. Nygaard), Oslo, 1956 (translated by Ragnar Christopherson)

Masini, L.V., *Art Nouveau*, Thames & Hudson, London, 1984

McKean, J. and Baxter, C., *Charles Rennie Mackintosh: Architect, Artist, Icon*, Lomond Books, Edinburgh, 2000

Mucha, S., *Alphonse Mucha*, Frances Lincoln Ltd, London, 2005

Néret, G., *Gustav Klimt*, Taschen, Köln, 1993

Ormiston, R., *Alphonse Mucha: Masterworks*, Flame Tree Publishing, London, 2007

Parry, L. (Ed.), *William Morris 1834–96*, Philip Wilson Publishers in association with V&A Publications, London, 1996, (exhibition catalogue)

Pevsner, N., *Pioneers of Modern Design*, Penguin Books, London, 1975

Rheims, M., *The Age of Art Nouveau*, Thames & Hudson, London, 1966

Robinson, M., *International Arts & Crafts*, Flame Tree Publishing, London, 2005

Robinson, M., *Millais & the Pre-Raphaelites*, Flame Tree Publishing, London, 2007

Robinson, M. and Ormiston, R., *Art Deco*, Flame Tree Publishing, London, 2008

Sainton, R., *Art Nouveau Posters and Graphics*, Academy Editions, London, 1977

Sembach, K.-J., *Art Nouveau*, Taschen, Köln, 1999

Solá-Morales, I., *Gaudí*, Ediciones Poligrafa, Barcelona, 1984 (translation by Kenneth Lyons)

Stevens, M. (Ed.), *Impressionism to Symbolism: The Belgian Avant-Garde 1880–1900*, Royal Academy of Arts Publications, London, 1994 (exhibition catalogue)

Watson, W., *The Great Japan Exhibition: Art of the Edo Period 1600–1868*, Royal Academy of Arts in association with Weidenfeld and Nicholson, London, 1981 (exhibition catalogue)

Acknowledgements

Rosalind Ormiston (Author)

Rosalind Ormiston is a lecturer at Kingston University, Surrey, where she teaches History of Art, Design and Architecture. Her specialist subjects include Classical Civilization, Renaissance Italy and Contemporary Architecture. She has lived in New York and Piedmont, Italy, and now divides her time between London, Cumbria and Italy. She writes features for both academic journals and consumer publications. She is currently researching Cumbrian architectural practice in the mid–late nineteenth century.

Michael Robinson (Author)

Michael Robinson is a freelance lecturer and writer on British art and design history. Originally an art dealer with his own provincial gallery in Sussex, he gained a first-class honours degree at Kingston University, Surrey. He is currently working on his doctorate, a study of early Modernist-period British dealers. He continues to lecture on British and French art of the Modern period.

Index